The 29th Division in warwickshire
and north Oxfordshire
December 1914 – March 1915

Before Gallipoli

Chris Holland

Foreword by
Professor Peter Simkins MBE, FRHistS

☙

2014

**Warwickshire Great War
Publications**

Cover design by Warwick Printing

Published by:
Warwickshire Great War Publications
Plott Bungalow, Plott Lane, Stretton on Dunsmore, Nr Rugby CV23 9HR, UK
Tel: +44 (0)2476 542493
Email: poors_plot@tiscali.co.uk

ISBN: 978-0-9574216-2-2

A CIP catalogue record for this book is available from the British Library

Printed and bound by:
Warwick Printing, Caswell Rd, Leamington Spa, Warwickshire, CV31 1QD

Contents

⁣

Acknowledgements

Nearly 10 years ago, Tony Jordan and I agreed to speak to the Stretton on Dunsmore History Society about the monument to the 29th Division, which lies within the parish. The occasion was to mark the 90th anniversary of the King's inspection of the Division in March 1915. Tony has a strong personal interest in the story because his parents met when his father, a soldier in the Royal Munster Fusiliers, was billeted with the 29th Division in Coventry in early 1915. For me, this was an early introduction to the many personal stories relating to the time that the 29th Division spent in the Warwickshire area, and to the impact of the soldiers' presence. It proved to be a bigger and more complex topic than I had imagined and its continuing fascination explains this present publication, an updating and expansion of a booklet called 'The Story Behind the Monument' that Tony and I produced in 2005. The principal difference is that the focus is now more on the local dimension, in keeping with the aims of Warwickshire Great War Publications to encourage and to publish research on the local impact of the Great War. It was Tony's knowledge and enthusiasm that helped stimulate my own interest and I am greatly indebted to him for that.

Many others have contributed stories and photos relating to members of their own families and I would particularly like to acknowledge the help of Jerry Ash, David Fordham, Anne Gore, the late Phil Heffer, Steve Jenkins and Derek Pheasant. The basis of the book, however, is information drawn from the resources held by the Warwickshire Library and Information Service, Banbury Library, the Warwickshire County Record Office, the Shakespeare Birthplace Trust, Leamington Spa Art Gallery and Museum and the Coventry History Centre. I would like to thank the staff and volunteers of those organisations for their assistance, which has included permission to use some of the photographs they hold. Further afield, resources held by the National Archives and in the Liddle Collection at Leeds University Library have also been used. The Cumbria Military Museum, the Essex Regiment Museum, the Hampshire Regiment Museum, the Worcestershire Regiment Museum, the Royal Dublin Fusiliers Association, the Royal Munster Fusiliers Association, the Gallipoli Association and Stretton on Dunsmore History Society have all been of considerable help.

David Fry and Albert Smith have been most generous in allowing me to draw on their extensive archives of photographs for the period and Paul Waller has also kindly allowed access to photographs and information that he holds, as has Alan Griffin. Stuart Mitchell has kindly permitted me to quote from his father's unpublished memoir about the stabling of the King's horses before the inspection. Peter Huxford has, once again, given freely of his time and ideas in checking through the text and suggesting improvements, as has Diane Holland. I would also like to acknowledge Allan Young, at Warwick Printing, for his expertise, patience and help in converting text and photos into a proper book.

In addition to those already mentioned, and those listed below in the illustrations section, the help, advice and interest of a good many others have been especially appreciated.

These include a number of people associated with the organisations mentioned above. Therefore, I would like to take the opportunity to thank the following: Chris Baker, Sam Collenette, Richard Davies, Stuart Eastwood, Lyn Edmonds, Louise Essex, Samantha Gray, Joanna Grindle, Helen Hargest, Ian Hook, Amy Hurst, Rob Langham, Anne Langley, David Llewellyn, Jean Prendergast, Martin Roberts, Vicki Slade and Foster Summerson – and, indeed, anyone else whose interest in the subject has helped to strengthen mine.

Finally, Peter Simkins very kindly agreed to write a Foreword to the book, despite the many demands that the approach of the centenary of the Great War have placed upon such a distinguished military historian; these include, of course, his Presidency of the Western Front Association.

Illustrations

I would like to acknowledge the following institutions and individuals for their kind permission in allowing me to reproduce photographs in their possession; copyright resides with them:

- Warwickshire Library and Information Service, Warwickshire County Council: No. 4, 26, 30, 48, 60, 70, 73, 75. These images are from the Local Studies Collection at Rugby Library.
- The Shakespeare Birthplace Trust: No. 16 (SC42 643), 22 (SC42 652), 27 (SC42 655), 43 (SC42 650), 44 (SC42 767), 55 (SC42 649), 63 (SC42 669).
- The Warwickshire County Record Office: No. 39 (PH (N) 759/68), 47 (PH 352/71/8), 51 (PH 350/820), 62 (PH352/135/146), 71 (PH350/2272).
- The Warwickshire County Record Office and the R.L. Graham Studio: No. 24 (CR 2555/211378.8).
- The Leamington Spa Art Gallery and Museum: No. 12 (LEAMG: M2099.1960 (69/18478).
- Coventry History Centre: No. 15 (C 01624), 20 (C 01630), 34 (C 01631), 53 (C 01625).
- Leeds University Library: No. 31 (GALL 067 Ollive, Lewis H.).
- Cumbria Military Museum: No. 3, 8, 57.
- The Essex Regiment Museum: No. 5, 6, 7.
- The Royal Dublin Fusiliers Association: No. 11, 56.
- The Worcestershire Regiment Museum: No. 74.
- Paul Waller: No. 13, 49, 50, 52.
- David Fry: No 2, 69, 78.
- David Fordham: No. 61, 64, 65.
- Alan Griffin: No. 35, 45.
- Dr Tadhg Moloney: No. 36, 37.
- Derek Pheasant: No. 9, 10.
- Albert Smith: No. 46, 72.
- Jerry Ash: No. 68.
- Gillian Ashley-Smith: 42.
- John Fortnum: No. 23.
- Phil Heffer: No. 14.
- Steve Jenkins: No. 32.
- Tony Jordan: No. 67.

In addition: photos No. 17, 18, 19, 21, 25, 28, 29, 33, 38, 40, 54, 58, 59 appeared in the *Coventry Graphic* for 1915 and I would like to acknowledge the help of the Herbert Art Gallery and Museum and the Coventry History Centre in enabling me to secure usable images from the newspaper.

Cover photos: No. 28 (*Coventry Graphic*), 32 (Steve Jenkins), 78 (David Fry)

Please note: every effort has been made to identify photographs that illustrate the range of units within the 29th Division, as well as the communities amongst whom they were billeted. However, this has not always proved successful and the balance is not entirely as I would have wished.

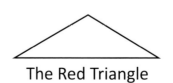

The Red Triangle

The distinctive narrow red triangle was the 29th Divisional sign. It was introduced by Major-General Sir Beauvoir de Lisle, GOC of the Division between June 1915 and March 1918. The purpose of the triangle, which is the ace of diamonds, cut in two along the diagonal, was to remind all ranks of the importance of the diamond as a military formation in open fighting, from a patrol to an army. Half of the diamond was worn on each shoulder of a soldier's uniform.

Foreword

ℭ

The last twenty years or so have seen a marked increase in the publication of new studies of British Army units that fought on the Western Front, or in other theatres of operations, during the Great War. Indeed, the numbers and frequency of such works which have appeared since the early 1990s now almost match the scale of the previous surge of unit histories produced in the decade immediately after the Armistice of November 1918. We can confidently expect an even bigger wave of fresh books of this type as we reach the Centenary of the First World War. Most of the new post-1990 studies, however, have focused upon individual infantry battalions, particularly 'Pals' and Territorial units with strong local links and identities. Books on larger formations such as divisions have been comparatively rare and few recently-published works in this field have examined the story of Regular divisions in the 1914-1918 conflict. One might also observe that, perhaps inevitably, the majority of recent battalion and divisional studies have tended to devote relatively little space to the unit's period of formation and training in the UK as compared with its active service in France or elsewhere.

Chris Holland's detailed and scholarly account of the time spent by the newly-assembled Regular 29th Division in the Midlands from January to March 1915, before it embarked for the Dardanelles, is therefore not only unusual but also extremely welcome, dealing as it does with the impact which the presence of large numbers of soldiers had upon various communities, and *vice versa*. As I remarked in my own book *Kitchener's Army* (Manchester University Press, 1988), the system of billeting troops upon the civilian population, as employed in Britain in the winter and spring of 1914-1915, brought the nation face to face with its Army to an unprecedented degree – probably only equalled as a social phenomenon in this country by the evacuation schemes of the Second World War. In my view, this billeting experiment was successful both because of the massive reservoir of goodwill that existed on both sides and because, above all, it helped to mobilise a colossal civilian effort in support of Britain's expanding Army, an effort which brought into play the vast network of voluntary organisations, charitable or otherwise, which permeated British society at the beginning of the Great War. One might argue that, at least in part, the fabric of British society is held together, and functions best, thanks to the willingness of bodies of volunteers who give up their spare time to attend meetings, seated around trestle tables in village and towns halls, or committee rooms, throughout the land. Chris Holland's empathetic study of the experience of the 29th Division in early 1915 skilfully captures the essence of this civilian effort and the interaction of the Army and society in the Midlands during the division's formative months, as its infantry and other ancillary units – drawn from scattered overseas garrisons – sought to become integrated into a true fighting body.

The huge losses suffered by the 29th Division on the Gallipoli peninsula and the Western Front meant that the formation was compelled to regenerate itself at least half a dozen times by November 1918. The original social and geographical composition and character of the division became increasingly diluted as the war progressed. Its experiences and combat record during and after the Gallipoli campaign were mixed. With the 1st Royal Newfoundland Regiment having replaced the 5th Royal Scots in September 1915, the division again incurred severe casualties at Beaumont Hamel on 1 July 1916, the first day of the Battle of the Somme. It subsequently distinguished itself at Monchy-le-Preux in April 1917, during the Battle of Arras, and saw further action during the Third Battle of Ypres and the Battle of Cambrai later that year. The following April it fought in the critical defensive battle on the Lys and played a worthy part in the final breakout from the Ypres Salient and the successful operations at Courtrai in September-October 1918. Whether or not it continued to merit Sir Ian Hamilton's 1915 description of it as 'incomparable' is open to debate. Certainly, consistently effective British formations such as the Guards Division, the 9th (Scottish) Division and the 18th (Eastern) Division would have felt that they had an equal or better claim to that title. However, the gallantry and devotion to duty of the 29th Division were never in doubt. This fine socio-military study of the division's early months is a valuable addition to the historiography of the British Army in the 1914-1918 conflict.

Professor Peter Simkins

January 2014

⚘

Introduction

cg

aptain Stair Gillon, in his history of the 29th Division, did not dwell long on the early part of 1915, when the Division was being formed in Warwickshire and north Oxfordshire. He dealt carefully with the 'order of battle' – the constituent parts of the Division, and their senior officers – and he paid generous tribute to "the kindly folk of the very heart of Old England", amongst whom most of the Division's soldiers had been billeted. "The troops were nearly all strangers to the district, but in a short time they were, and remained, on the best terms with their entertainers. They were much missed when they went away." He also expressed regret that the dispersal of the Division over a large area, as well as the nature of the local countryside, meant that practically no divisional, and very little brigade, training could be accomplished. But, on the whole, he concluded that: "The life of a regular division prior to embarkation has little interest for the general reader." Indeed, he felt that only two incidents were worthy of mention. One of these, not surprisingly, was the inspection of the Division by King George V, on 12th March, 1915; the other, and the one he chose to mention first, was the inoculation against enteric fever (typhoid) of over 99% of the force.[1]

When one considers the substance of Stair Gillon's story, it is hardly surprising that he did not spend long on "The Birth of the Division". The 29th Division fought throughout the Gallipoli campaign, before being transferred to the Western Front. It had the unenviable distinction of being the only British division to be involved in both the first day of the landings on the Gallipoli Peninsula, in 1915, and the first day of the Battle of the Somme, in 1916. On the first occasion it suffered more than 3,000 casualties; on the second, more than 5,000. The Division's involvement on the Somme continued into the autumn of 1916. In 1917, it took part in the Battles of Arras, 3rd Ypres and Cambrai and, in 1918, in the Battles of the Lys and the fighting in Flanders that was part of the 'Advance to Victory'. The Division's soldiers won 27 VCs during the war, the highest number for any division. When the Division embarked for active service, its strength was 19,000; Captain Gillon estimated the Division's total casualties during the war – killed, wounded, sick and prisoners of war – as "something like 94,000. Gallipoli alone accounted for 34,000." Put another way: between the Division's first losses in combat, following the attack on the transport ship *Manitou* (17th April, 1915) and the Armistice, the 29th Division suffered an average of some 500 casualties per week. It was hardly surprising that Captain Gillon subtitled his book "A Record of Gallant Deeds" and the Division earned its appellations "Incomparable" and "Immortal".

However, it is the contention of this short book that the time which the 29th Division spent in Warwickshire and north Oxfordshire is of greater interest and, in some ways, of greater importance than Captain Gillon made out. The most famous incident was, of course, the King's inspection of the Division, although rather surprisingly – and in marked contrast to other aspects of the Division's stay in the area – the inspection was little reported at the time. Nor should one belittle the importance of inoculation against typhoid fever, given the large number of deaths caused by the disease: of the British Force that served in South Africa during the Second Anglo-Boer War, 1899-1902, more than 8,000 died of typhoid, a larger number than were killed in action.[2] But there is much more to the story of the 29th Division's time in the Midlands than simply these "two incidents".

Billeting ensured that the 29th Division left for active service in good health and with high morale – of considerable value in the struggles to come and, as will be argued, in marked contrast to two of the other divisions formed from units withdrawn from the Empire. For the great majority of the 29th Division's soldiers it was an enjoyable and comfortable interlude, and one upon which the perils and hardships of the Gallipoli campaign would quickly confer a nostalgic sheen: "dear old Rugby", "who of the Battalion will ever forget Leamington?", "it was a sad day when we left Kenilworth", "we were always made at home wherever we went". For many of the soldiers, the relationships formed with local girls were no doubt casual, at least to them, but for others they were of more lasting importance. A number married and others entered into 'understandings', to be furthered when the soldiers returned from war. Many of these relationships would, of course, be tragically brief but some of the 29th settled in the area after the war; others, no doubt, took their brides to different parts of the country. There were also ordinary friendships formed with local people – often the families upon whom men had been billeted, or resulting from involvement in local churches and other organisations. These were sometimes maintained for many years.

For the area, the presence of the 29th Division, however brief, was a matter of consequence. Setting aside the personal stories, billeting gave a timely economic boost to a number of towns and larger villages. It briefly brought life back to communities that had been deprived of many of their young men through enlistment in the armed forces. It also changed perspectives:

> "The town does not appear the same, and military life is for the moment uppermost. The one thought that is dominant is the war, and the soldiers in our midst. ... There is a suddenness about military life which causes one to be ready for anything and everything. It has been an unique experience for the town, and whilst it has certainly upset the normal life of the people, it has given an intensity and meaning to our thoughts, especially on the war. The pathos and tragedy of it all has been brought more vividly before our minds ..."[3]

In Peter Simkins' words, billeting meant that "the nation came face to face with its army"[4] and, in the case of the soldiers of the 29th Division, the Warwickshire area was favourably impressed. As early as 26th March, 1915, and within days of the 29th Division's departure, the *Coventry Graphic* reported a proposal for a memorial stone to be placed on the spot where the King inspected the 29th Division.

Local people had quickly identified with men whom they often came to regard as "our soldiers" – to the irritation of many of the local soldiers who were then on the Western Front or in training in the United Kingdom. There seems little doubt that the heavy losses suffered by the 29th Division were keenly felt in the area and that they strengthened the determination to create a lasting memorial. Despite the considerable cost of the numerous local memorials that were erected in the immediate post-war period, the necessary money was found. It paid for the handsome obelisk, which stands "where Telford's coaching road is crossed by the Roman Fosse Way", and which marks the saluting point on 12th March, 1915; and it paid for the replanting of the avenue of trees that had overlooked the line of inspection. Understandably, the inscription on the monument pays tribute to the 29th Division's "incomparable services" during the war; more simply, it also commemorates "their stay in Warwickshire".

HERE
IN THE CENTRE OF ENGLAND
WHERE TELFORD'S COACHING-ROAD
FROM LONDON TO HOLYHEAD
. IS CROSSED BY THE ROMAN FOSSE WAY
ON THE 12TH OF MARCH 1915
HIS MAJESTY KING GEORGE V
REVIEWED HIS TROOPS
OF THE IMMORTAL
XXIX·DIVISION
SHORTLY BEFORE THEY EMBARKED
FOR ACTIVE SERVICE
IN GALLIPOLI

IN MEMORY OF THEIR·STAY IN WARWICKSHIRE
1914-15 AND OF THEIR INCOMPARABLE SERVICES
SINCE THE AVENUE ON THIS ROAD WAS REPLANTED
AND THIS MONUMENT ERECTED BY
INHABITANTS·OF·THE·COUNTY.

1. *The dedication on the monument to the 29th Division.* (© Author)

[1] Captain Stair Gillon, "The Story of the 29th Division: A Record of Gallant Deeds"; Thomas Nelson & Sons, 1925
[2] Professor J.C. de Villiers, "The Medical Aspects of the Anglo-Boer War, 1899-1902, Part II"; Journal of The South African Military History Society, Vol. 6, No. 3, June 1984. "The official figures reveal that, of the British Force of 556,653 men who served in the Anglo-Boer War, 57,684 contracted typhoid, 8,225 of whom died, while 7,582 were killed in action."
[3] *Nuneaton Observer*, 5th March, 1915, quoting from the 'Baptist Magazine' for March
[4] Peter Simkins, "Kitchener's Army"; Manchester University Press, 1988

1

The Inspection: 12th March, 1915

୧୪

On 12th March, 1915, the 29th Division demonstrated its readiness for war. A little over two months after being mobilised, it awaited the King's inspection before departing on active service. It was the last of Britain's regular army divisions to be formed in the Great War.* Twelve infantry battalions, the Divisional artillery brigades that had been billeted in the area, as well as "representative parties of other units",[1] assembled along the London Road between its intersection with the Fosse Way, near Stretton on Dunsmore, and the railway station at Dunchurch. They were drawn up on the broad verge, on the northern side of the road, a line of review that was some two miles long. On the far right of the line – the part closest to the crossroads – were the mounted troops and the artillery; on the far left, the 88th Infantry Brigade. By far the largest component was made up the infantry and they assembled in numerical order of brigade (86th, 87th, 88th).†

It was mid-morning when the royal party arrived at Dunchurch station and mounted the horses that were waiting for them. King George V was accompanied by Major Wigram, Lieutenant-Colonel Dugdale and Vice-Admiral Keppel. On leaving the station, the royal party rode slowly down the ranks of soldiers, who came to attention as the King approached. The infantry were lined up four deep, facing the road; the artillery faced in the direction from which the King was coming, even though this would mean that the horses and limbers would have to be turned before they could proceed to the inspection point. As each regiment was passed, its colonel walked by the King's side.

The King reached the crossroads at about 12.15 p.m. Remaining mounted, he took up a position on the south side, from which he would receive the salute. This was on a triangle of grass, where the road turned towards Stretton on Dunsmore. The King's arrival was cheered by the crowd, estimated by Henry Wilkins, a local journalist, at just over a thousand strong, and also by the Warwickshire Yeomanry, who occupied the north-east corner of the crossroads. Colonel Wyley, the High Sheriff of Warwickshire, and Captain Brinkley, the Chief Constable of the County, were among those present.[2] The Division then proceeded to march down the London Road and past the King.

---

* Although several of the Division's units came from the Territorial Force, the 29th Division is still regarded as belonging to the regular army and listed as such in the Order of Battle of Divisions.

† Given the traditions of the British Army, it would be reasonable to assume that the battalions in each brigade were arranged in order of precedence. This is the order shown on the diagram on Page 30. (The 5th Royal Scots, as the only Territorial battalion, was the junior battalion, although the Regiment enjoyed seniority over the others represented in the 29th Division.) However, Oswin Creighton states that, when he joined the line of review, "I sat on my horse just between the R.F.s [Royal Fusiliers] and the Munsters". This would suggest that precedence was not strictly adhered to, at least in the 86th Brigade.

2. *King George V, mounted on 'Delhi', leaving Dunchurch Station with his entourage on the morning of 12ᵗʰ March, 1915.* (© David Fry)

Although not part of the 29ᵗʰ Division, the Warwickshire Yeomanry led the march-past and the first officers to give the salute were the Yeomanry's Colonel Charteris and Major Lord Willoughby de Broke. Then came the Division's artillery "in column of route", followed by the other divisional troops, and finally by the infantry in double fours (eight abreast). Stair Gillon later described "twelve splendid battalions, each at war strength in personnel, with fixed bayonets, filling the broad roadway from edge to edge and constantly flowing onwards under the canopy of gigantic elm trees";[3] Oswin Creighton recorded "the long line of silver bayonets winding through the trees like a stream".[4] All proceeded smoothly, although, as Gillon pointed out, a considerable strain was placed on the brigade on the extreme left (the 88ᵗʰ), who had to gain about 2,500 yards to get into the correct formation.

The King returned the salute of every officer and the Division marched in quick time, to the music of the regimental bands and the corps of pipes and drums. The march-past took until 1.23 p.m., according to Henry Wilkins. The band then played the National Anthem and, to the accompaniment of more cheering, the King began his journey back to Dunchurch, ignoring the waiting motor cars in favour of a canter along the road's grass verge. The King was in good humour, impressed as he had been by "my British Division from India". Once the units got clear of the saluting point, they returned, by pre-arranged routes, to their billeting areas.

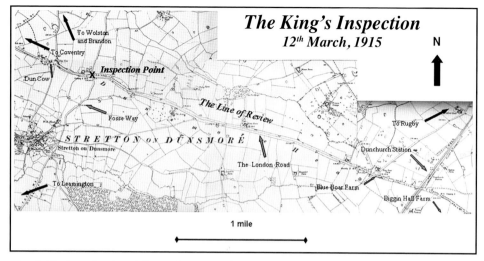

Map 1: The line of review, 12th March, 1915.

It must have been the biggest concentration of soldiers in Warwickshire since the Battle of Edgehill in 1642 and the King was not the only one to have been impressed. Captain Gillon thought it was "a splendid spectacle"; Captain Clement Milward recorded "guns and horses in beautiful condition and the infantry incomparable";[5] to Oswin Creighton the Division "seemed vast, and the men were magnificent". Even Lieutenant Guy Nightingale, who appears not to have enjoyed the occasion very much, admitted that the Division "looked a fine crowd".[6] The great avenue of trees bordering the London Road, which had been planted in the eighteenth century by John, Duke of Montagu ("John the Planter"), clearly added to the sense of theatre.[‡]

But what were the opinions of the ordinary soldiers? For the most part, their views can only be surmised. Those billeted in Rugby would have had a relatively short march to the London Road; those from Coventry somewhat longer: Guy Nightingale, Royal Munster Fusiliers, complained of a march of eight and half miles, along "a beastly hard road". The Rev. Oswin Creighton, Chaplain to the 86th Brigade, started from Coventry at 7.30 a.m., and joined up with the 2nd Battalion Royal Fusiliers, "who had started very early" from their billets in the city. He estimated the march as seven or eight miles. By contrast, the 1st Battalion Royal Dublin Fusiliers were conveyed by train from Kenilworth to Brandon, with only a short march to follow.[7] The Lancashire Fusiliers must have enjoyed similar assistance: leaving Nuneaton at 8 a.m., they were in position to be inspected by the King at 11.40 a.m.[8] Of the battalions of the 88th Brigade, now concentrated in Leamington and Warwick, the 5th Battalion Royal Scots took the train to Dunchurch and the 2nd Battalion Hampshire Regiment also went by train and then marched back to Warwick.[9] Presumably, the other two battalions in the Brigade enjoyed similar help on the journey out. However, it would seem likely that the artillery units from Leamington would have come by road, bringing with them their horses and limbers, although not their guns. According to Creighton, the soldiers had not been officially told that the King was coming, although they must soon have guessed the purpose of the occasion.

[‡] However, looking back nearly 60 years later, R. B. Gillett, in 1915 a young and inexperienced 2nd Lieutenant in the 2nd Battalion Hampshire Regiment, only remembered the location of the King's inspection as a "a country lane". (Gillett, R.B.: transcript of interview with Peter Liddle, 1973; Liddle Collection, Leeds University Library, GS 0624)

Henry Wilkins described the day as fine but without sun, a description that accords with the photographs of the occasion. Guy Nightingale mentioned a long wait in the cold, presumably the experience of many that morning. Did the field kitchens accompany the soldiers who had marched or did the men have to make do with rations they carried? There are a good many things about the arrangements that day that are not known but one can imagine the troops waiting, with various degrees of patience, for the King's arrival, some grumbling, some no doubt pulling aside to the field hedges and ditches to relieve themselves. But professional soldiers, who made up the great majority of those present, would have been accustomed to such occasions and to enforced idleness, most recently on their long sea-journeys back from the Empire. As the King's party approached, they would have come smartly to attention and, when the time came, they would have marched to the inspection point with the precision that their training and regimental pride dictated. Private H. Harris of the 87th Field Ambulance later recalled that, by the time of the march past, he and his fellow Territorials were "tired and foot weary", after their march from Rugby. "The drum and fife band of the 1st Border Regiment, however, provided a much needed stimulus and the unit marched past as smartly as the regulars."[10]

There can be no doubting the soldiers' pride in their regiments. Did they also now feel a loyalty to the 29th Division, a military unit that had only come into existence in January? Perhaps not: 12th March was the first occasion the Division had come together and its soldiers could not have known its illustrious and costly future. But, as the Division wound its way down the London Road, the soldiers must have sensed its strength and potential, and that must also have influenced their mood. In the parlance of a later age, they were good and they knew it. "A more impressive spectacle than the march past of those regular soldiers with fixed bayonets it would be hard to imagine", was Private Harris's conclusion.[11] More simply, Bandsman H. Brown, 1st Battalion Lancashire Fusiliers, recorded the occasion in his diary as a "grand sight".[12]

3. *George V reviewing the 1st Battalion Border Regiment; London Road, 12th March, 1915.*
(© Cumbria Military Museum)

4. *The King and his entourage at the saluting point, as the Divisional artillery passes down the verge of the London Road; 12th March, 1915. Seemingly an amateur photographer's shot, taken above the heads of the crowd.* (© Warwickshire Library and Information Service)

Within days of the inspection, the Division's soldiers were leaving the area, bound for Avonmouth and the transports that would take them to the Mediterranean. On 25th April, just over six weeks after the inspection, the Division landed on the defended coast of the Gallipoli Peninsula, suffering heavy casualties in the process. When the Division finally withdrew from Gallipoli in January 1916, comparatively few of the 19,000 who had sailed from England were left unscathed. Yet the Gallipoli campaign was only the start of the 29th Division's war.

In August, a resident in Clifton Road, Rugby, received a letter from one of the officers of the Border Regiment, Captain F.H.S. Le Mesurier. Wounded twice in the fighting at Gallipoli, Le Mesurier was in a sombre mood when he wrote from hospital in London. He had already lost his younger brother and a cousin, killed in the Persian Gulf and France, respectively, and "the loss of so many brother officers and good comrades [at Gallipoli] has upset us all". Looking back, the weeks the Battalion spent in Rugby stood out as "quite the happiest time of our lives" and the events of 12th March, 1915, appeared in a new light: "The march past of the 29th Division before the King was truly similar to that of the 'Old Guard' before Napoleon, before they marched to certain death at Waterloo."[13]

BUCKINGHAM PALACE

Message from the King to the 29th Division
March 12th, 1915

I was much struck with the steadiness under arms and the marching powers of the splendid body of men composing the 29th Division.

The combination of so many experienced officers and seasoned soldiers, whom I particularly noticed on parade, will, I feel confident, prove of inestimable value on the field of battle.

That the 29th Division, wherever employed, will uphold the high reputation already won by my army in France and Belgium, I have no doubt.

Rest assured that your movements and welfare will ever be in my thoughts.

"The King sent us a very nice little message." (Oswin Creighton)

ℭঝ

1   Captain Stair Gillon: "The Story of the 29th Division"; Thomas Nelson and Sons Ltd, 1925

2   Henry Charles Wilkins: "Journal of the Great European War"; Coventry History Centre, JN940.3

3   Captain Stair Gillon: op cit

4   Rev. Oswin Creighton: "With the 29th Division at Gallipoli"; Longmans, Green and Co., 1916

5   Lieutenant-General Sir Clement Milward: Journal and Diaries; National Army Museum; quoted in Michael Hickey "Gallipoli"; John Murray, 1995

6   Guy Nightingale Papers: National Archives PRO 30/71; Diary January-December 1915, PRO 30/71/5

7   Colonel H.C. Wylly: "Neill's 'Blue Caps', Vol. 3, 1914-1922"; Gale & Polden Ltd, 1923

8   Brown, H: diary; Liddle Collection, Leeds University Library, GALL 015

9   McKay, George: diary; Liddle Collection, Leeds University Library, GALL 058 and Gillett, R.B.: diary; Liddle Collection, Leeds University Library, GALL 0624. McKay was a Bandsman in the 5th Royal Scots and Gillett a 2nd Lieutenant in the 2nd Hampshire Regiment.

10 Harris, H.: memoirs; Liddle Collection, Leeds University Library, GALL (REC) 161. Harris was a Private in the 87th Field Ambulance, a Territorial unit.

11 Harris, H.; op cit

12 Brown, H.; op cit

13 *Rugby Advertiser*, 14th August, 1915

2

The 29th Division and the 'Heart of England'

CB

By way of explanation

Although there is an obvious connection between the King's inspection of the 29th Division and the location of the subsequent monument to the Division, it may still seem strange that the Division was in the Warwickshire area in the first place. There was no pre-war link between the Division and the area, for the simple reason that the Division did not exist until it was created in the early part of 1915. The units that made up this new Division were associated with many different parts of the United Kingdom but none with Warwickshire or Oxfordshire. Moreover, the exploits that made the 29th Division famous were achieved overseas, in theatres of war, which is where divisional memorials are nearly always found.

To understand how the link between the Warwickshire area and the 29th Division was formed, it is necessary to touch briefly on the organisation of the British Army in 1914, on the effect of the early losses suffered by the British Expeditionary Force in France and Flanders, and on the chronic shortage of accommodation for soldiers in the United Kingdom during the winter of 1914-15.

The active strength of Britain's regular army in August 1914 was just under 250,000. Of this total, a significant proportion (a little over 46%) was serving in the Empire and included 74 infantry battalions and 12 cavalry regiments.[1] Predictably, the largest concentrations were the British garrisons in India and Burma, which comprised 52 infantry battalions: 17 quartered in Bengal, 14 in the Punjab, 12 in Bombay, 6 in Madras and 3 in Burma.[2]

The distribution of Britain's professional army reflected the importance of Britain's imperial commitments, whilst its organisation owed much to the army reforms designed by Lord Cardwell in the 1880s. As a result of these reforms, nearly all the infantry regiments with county or regional associations operated a two-battalion system for their regular soldiers, with one battalion overseas and the other at home training recruits and providing drafts (replacements) for the overseas battalion. Periodically, the overseas battalion would exchange places with the home battalion.[*] Although there were variations, the normal terms of service for soldiers by 1914 were seven years with the Colours and five on the Reserve. Following an initial period of service at home, a soldier would normally expect to spend the bulk of his time in the army overseas.

---

[*] A small number of regiments had a pre-war strength of four regular battalions, rather than two. One of these was the Worcestershire Regiment, which is why the 4th Battalion Worcestershire Regiment, subsequently part of the 29th Division, belonged to the regular army.

One consequence of this system was that most home battalions were well below establishment (their optimum number) when war broke out and heavily dependent on young soldiers, often with no more than two years service, as well as reservists to make up their numbers. Although these battalions performed gallantly in the British Expeditionary Force (BEF) that was sent out to France, there was clearly a strong argument for re-calling the overseas units, with their complement of seasoned regulars.

This argument was further strengthened by the heavy losses suffered by the BEF on the Western Front in 1914, notably at Mons and Le Cateau, in the Battle of the Aisne, and in the 1st Battle of Ypres. By the end of the year, the BEF had suffered almost 90,000 casualties – killed, wounded and missing. These early engagements quickly drew in the 10% of reinforcements, which had been initially held at the base camps in France, as well as the remainder of the reservists at home. So great were the losses that some of the half-trained Territorial units, which were originally intended for home defence, had to be sent to France as reinforcements.

However, many of the overseas battalions could not be recalled immediately, as second line battalions had to be sent out to protect Britain's imperial interests. Some of battalions from India proceeded directly to France, along with two divisions of the Indian Corps. Some of the other recalled battalions formed the basis of the 7th and 8th Divisions, which went to the Western Front in October and November 1914. Those infantry battalions returning to the United Kingdom during the later part of 1914 and the early part of 1915 were used to create three new divisions. As the divisional numbers 9 to 26 had now been allocated to the New Army (the so-called 'Kitchener Volunteers'), these new divisions were numbered 27, 28 and 29. Not all of their units were made up of regular soldiers (and this included one of the infantry battalions in the 29th Division); nonetheless, these divisions were regarded as part of the regular army. They were the last regular divisions to be created in the Great War and the 29th Division – the final one of these to be sent into combat – was therefore "the veritable last of Britain's Regular Army".[3]

By the time the last of the overseas battalions returned home, Great Britain must have seemed awash with soldiers. In addition to soldiers of the Territorial Force still in the United Kingdom, there were more than a million men who had answered Kitchener's call for volunteers and who were now under training. Accommodation had to be found for all of them. The small size of Britain's pre-war army stationed at home meant that army barracks were insufficient for this purpose, even when the allowance of space per man had been reduced by a third. A programme of hut building had been started but had run into difficulties and those living under canvas often faced appalling conditions, especially after the weather broke in mid-October 1914.

The pressure was eased by the billeting of some 800,000 soldiers on the civilian population during the winter of 1914-15. So it was that soldiers who would help create the 29th Division were allocated to billets in Warwickshire and north Oxfordshire. The main conurbations outside of Birmingham were used to accommodate them, with two infantry battalions going to Nuneaton and one to nearby Stockingford, two to Coventry, one to Stratford-upon-Avon, two to Banbury and three to Rugby. (The Division's other infantry battalion, the 5th Royal Scots, a Territorial unit, only arrived in the area in March.) The Division's Headquarters were at Leamington, which also hosted the Divisional artillery. Coventry, Nuneaton and Rugby were used to billet companies of the Royal Army Medical Corps and some of the smaller towns and villages, such as Kenilworth, Kineton, Southam and Barford, also took units, for example companies of the Royal Engineers and of the Army Service Corps.

It is probably no longer possible to calculate the exact number of the 29th Division's troops who were billeted in Warwickshire and north Oxfordshire. Not all of the Division's units came to the area and the numbers of those who were present varied over time,

Map 2: The billeting area.

with the support units generally arriving later than the artillery and infantry. Nor were the units necessarily at full strength when they first arrived: most infantry battalions, for example, seem to have been at least 10% below establishment. Fresh drafts therefore came into the area over the weeks that followed. There was also some movement out of the area, as a relatively small number of soldiers were deemed unfit for active service or a few officers were promoted to other units. Perhaps 10,000-11,000, out of the 19,000 who would eventually make up the 29th Division, were present in the area by mid-January, with that number increasing to more than 17,000 by the time that the Division departed for Avonmouth in the third week of March.

There seems little doubt that the presence of the 29th Division had an impact upon the area in which it was billeted. However, was the reverse also the case – did billeting have any real effect upon the Division? Arguably, it did. The Division enjoyed good accommodation during its time in the Midlands and the importance of this is clearly illustrated by the contrasting experiences of both the 27th and 28th Divisions, made up, like the 29th Division, of regular battalions withdrawn from the Empire.

The 27th and 28th Divisions

The returning soldiers who made up the 27th Division were given little time to recover and adjust to winter conditions in Europe before they were despatched to France in December 1914. The Division sustained heavy casualties during the desperate fighting in the 2nd Battle of Ypres, in April and May 1915, and was subsequently withdrawn from the Western Front later that year.[4] On their arrival in England, the 28th Division's battalions were put into camps around Winchester, where they stayed in December and January, before embarking for France between 15th and 18th January. Their time in England was spent largely under canvas in appalling conditions. On 1st January, 1915, their Commanding Officer, General Sir Edward Bulfin, wrote:

> "The condition of the Camps is deplorable ... Owing to the continuous rain the tent bottoms in some cases are afloat. I have ordered 50% of the men to go on three days furlo' at once and the remainder to move today into billets in Winchester. ... Today there is not a man with a dry suit of clothes on him and the Camp is one huge quagmire with men and horses wading about. I am putting this Brigade [85th] to-night into billets. I need not tell you the difficulties of mobilising are very great – blankets, clothing, saddlery – all are soaking wet."[5]

Such conditions had a damaging effect on the training of the newly-formed 28th Division and presumably on its morale. These problems were compounded by the Division's early experiences on the Western Front during 1915, which were sufficiently unfortunate that, at one point, Sir John French took the drastic step of temporarily exchanging the 28th Division's Brigades with experienced ones from the 3rd and 5th Divisions. The Brigades were returned shortly before the 2nd Battle of Ypres, during which the 28th Division suffered heavy casualties. In October 1915, the 28th Division was also withdrawn from the Western Front and sent to Salonika, where it was joined in early 1916 by the 27th Division. Both divisions remained on this front for the rest of the war.

The contrast with the formation of the 29th Division could not have been greater. Of the time the Border Regiment spent in Rugby, for example, it has been written:

> "The men were billeted in the town and were royally treated by the citizens. They were lucky not to be in some freezing hutted camp, but could become acclimatised from the heat of Burma in warm houses. ... The Regiment was very happy in Rugby where the inhabitants were full of kindness and hospitality."[6] [†]

When it left the Midlands, the Division's soldiers were fit and their morale was high. Despite heavy losses, first at Gallipoli and then on the Western Front, the record of the 29th Division was to be one of the most distinguished in the Great War. Whereas the 27th and 28th Divisions became, in Martin Middlebrook's words, "two of the almost 'forgotten' divisions of the war",[7] the 29th Division earned the appellation "Immortal".

☙

[†] However, not all of the 29th Division were as fortunate. For example, the Divisional Ammunition Column (DAC) did not come to the Midlands but was based at Slough, where it found that billets in private houses had already been taken and its men had to make do with empty properties. This may help explain the problem that the DAC had at this time with men going absent without leave, to which the proximity of London and cheap rail fares also contributed. Finding stabling was another problem and horses were left in "swamped fields". In early March, the DAC left for Taunton, where it briefly enjoyed better billets, before embarkation from Avonmouth. (War Diary of the 29th Divisional Ammunition Column; National Archives WO 95/4308)

---

[1]   Charles Messenger: "Call-To-Arms"; Weidenfeld & Nicolson, 2005
[2]   Colonel H.C. Wylly: "The Border Regiment in the Great War"; Gale & Polden, 1924; Charles Messenger gives the figure as 51 infantry battalions.
[3]   Martin Middlebrook: "Your Country Needs You"; Pen & Sword Books Ltd, 2000
[4]   See Charles Messenger: op cit
[5]   National Archives PRO 30/57/51; quoted in "Call-To-Arms" by Charles Messenger: op cit
[6]   Ralph May with Stuart Eastwood and Clive Elderton: "Glory Is No Compensation"; Silver Link Publishing Ltd, 2003
[7]   Martin Middlebrook: op cit. However, Martin Middlebrook pays full tribute to the self-sacrifice of the 27th and 28th Divisions in the 2nd Battle of Ypres.

3

'Tommy Atkins'

⊂ℨ

The overseas battalions

It is highly likely that the people in the Warwickshire area would have extended a warm welcome to any troops who were billeted upon them in early 1915. However, there seems little doubt that the appeal of the 29th Division's soldiers was significantly increased by the fact that the great majority of them were professional soldiers returning from the Empire. They were: "a fine lot physically and very smart", "well-seasoned troops", "a fine stalwart lot of fellows", "sunburnt Irishmen" – and so on. Inevitably, there were initial concerns about how regular army soldiers might behave but these were soon dispelled by men who seemed to bring with them some of the aura and fascination of the East. They also belonged to regiments with distinctive identities that owed much to service overseas.

Some of the infantry battalions that would make up the 29th Division had arrived in the Empire a relatively short time before their recall. Others, however, had been overseas for a good many years. The 4th Battalion Worcestershire Regiment, for example, had gone to Malta in 1906, before moving on to India in 1909; in August 1914, it was stationed in Upper Burma. Another battalion in Burma when war broke out was the 1st Battalion Border Regiment and it can serve as a brief example of the life of an overseas battalion.[1]

Like the Worcesters, the 1st Battalion Border Regiment had left the United Kingdom in 1906. For two years the Battalion was stationed at Gibraltar, where it was still technically the Regiment's Home Battalion, and therefore providing drafts for the 2nd Battalion in South Africa. In the autumn of 1908, the 1st Battalion left Gibraltar for India, before moving to Burma in the autumn of 1910. After a spell at Rangoon, it was then sent to Maymyo, in Upper Burma, in April 1912, though detachments served in other parts of the country.

Whilst helping maintain a British presence in the Empire, the 1st Battalion Border Regiment spent much of its time training, within the physical limitations of the locality, such as jungle in Burma, and at sport. Both officers and men were encouraged to participate in sport and overseas battalions often produced sportsmen and teams of a high standard in a wide variety of sports, including soccer, rugby, cricket, hockey, cross-country running, athletics and boxing. Whilst at Rangoon, some of the officers of the Border Regiment even enjoyed success at rowing. Social life could be active, though the onus was often on providing entertainments from within a battalion's resources, through concerts and the like, while the mess was central to the lives of the officers. Some soldiers and a few officers had wives and children with them, though marriage was generally discouraged and there were no marriage allowances. Overseas battalions, like the 1st Battalion Border Regiment, could develop high levels of efficiency and a very strong 'esprit de corps', with an intense loyalty to the regiment, in turn, reflecting the county or regional associations implicit in the regimental system of the time.

The 1st Battalion Essex Regiment at Mauritius before the outbreak of war:

5. *The infantry barracks.* (© Essex Regiment Museum)

6. *Christmas church parade.* (© Essex Regiment Museum)

7. *The officers' mess.* (© Essex Regiment Museum)

Battalions that were overseas for several years could see a considerable turnover in personnel, as some men returned home on completion of their service, to be replaced by drafts from the home battalion. However, other soldiers would choose to re-engage. When the overseas units that formed the basis of the 29th Division reached Warwickshire, they contained in their ranks a number of men who had been overseas for a considerable time. Some of the Munster Fusiliers, for example, had not been back to the United Kingdom for 15 years or more, whilst two of the Royal Fusiliers who arrived at Stockingford, on 11th January, had only seen England for the first time when they arrived at Avonmouth the previous day, having been born and raised in the Empire. Similarly, eight members of the Royal Artillery billeted in Leamington were born in India and had never been to England.[2]

The units that were being withdrawn from the Empire in the autumn of 1914 therefore contained a great many officers and men of some maturity. Analysis, for example, of Commonwealth War Graves Commission information on members of the 1st Battalion Lancashire Fusiliers who fell on 25th and 26th April, 1915, the first two days of the Gallipoli campaign, reveals an average age of 26 (for those whose age is recorded). Seasoned soldiers were often no angels but most knew how to conduct themselves. The regard for the 1st Battalion Border Regiment was such that when they left Maymyo, in Burma, in November 1914, they were cheered on their way by large crowds of well-wishers, in scenes not dissimilar to those that would be witnessed in March 1915, when the Border Regiment and other units left their billeting areas in Warwickshire and north Oxfordshire.

29th Division: distribution of overseas battalions in August 1914

India:
- 1st Bn Royal Dublin Fusiliers: had been at Madras for 18 months and in India for more than four and a half years;
- 2nd Bn Hampshire Regiment was stationed at Mhow, having been in India for 8 months;
- 1st Bn King's Own Scottish Borderers was stationed at Lucknow;
- 1st Bn Lancashire Fusiliers was stationed at Karachi;
- 2nd Bn of the Royal Fusiliers was stationed at Calcutta;
- 1st Bn Royal Inniskilling Fusiliers was stationed at Trimulgherry.

Burma:
- 1st Bn Border Regiment was stationed at Maymyo, in Upper Burma, having moved from Gibraltar in October 1908;
- 4th Bn Worcestershire Regiment had moved in 1909 to Bareilly in India, after three years at Malta, and from there to Meiktila in Upper Burma;
- 1st Bn Royal Munster Fusiliers had five companies at Rangoon, two at Thayetmyo and one at Port Blair in the Andaman Islands.

Mauritius / South Africa:
- 1st Bn Essex Regiment was split up. In November 1913, half the Battalion, along with the Battalion Headquarters, had left Karachi and sailed to Mauritius, whilst the other half of the Battalion went on to Durban in South Africa.

China:
- 2nd Bn South Wales Borderers was stationed at Tientsin.

8. *Soldiers of the 1ˢᵗ Battalion Border Regiment about to depart from Maymyo Station, Burma, on their way back to England; 19ᵗʰ November, 1914.* (© Cumbria Military Museum)

A Soldier of the Empire:
Company Sergeant Major Bernard Steven, 1ˢᵗ Battalion Essex Regiment

Although born near Wrexham, in North Wales, Bernard Steven initially enlisted in the Essex Yeomanry, in February 1902, at the age of 19. He appears to have acquired a taste for military life, because he then joined the regular army at Warley Barracks, Brentwood, in December 1902, and became a Private in the 1ˢᵗ Battalion Essex Regiment. He immediately left for India, where he served for the next eight years, his postings taking him to many of the garrison towns of India and Burma. A photograph of him in 1906, following his promotion to Corporal, shows him as "the very epitome of the soldier of Empire"*: ramrod straight and with waxed moustache, and yet still only in his mid 20s. In 1910, by now Sergeant Steven, he came back to England and married Annie Eley, before returning to India with his wife. Their first child was born at Quetta, a garrison town near the North West Frontier. When war broke out, Sergeant Steven was with the half of the Battalion that was stationed on Mauritius and which returned from there to England. Annie and their two children must also have returned home because another photograph shows the family in England in early 1915. Whether Annie travelled with the 1ˢᵗ Battalion or separately is not known. By the time the Battalion left for Gallipoli, Bernard had been promoted to the rank of Company Sergeant Major.

9. *The "very epitome of the soldier of Empire": Corporal Bernard Steven, 1ˢᵗ Battalion Essex Regiment, in 1906.*
(© Derek Pheasant)

10. *Company Sergeant Major Bernard Steven, his wife, Annie, and children; early 1915.*
(© Derek Pheasant)

* Derek Pheasant, to whom I am indebted for this information on his maternal grandparents.

The return of the overseas units

The process by which the overseas units that were to make up the 29th Division were withdrawn from Empire and made their way to the Midlands was a lengthy one. It appears to have begun with the artillery and the recall of two batteries from the Royal Horse Artillery and three from the Royal Field Artillery that had been serving in India. Although it is not known when they were withdrawn, the RFA batteries were stationed at Winchester by November. The withdrawal of the infantry battalions began in October 1914 and concluded with arrival of the 4th Battalion Worcestershire Regiment in early February 1915. The journeys could be protracted: for example, the 1st Battalion Royal Munster Fusiliers took nearly 12 weeks to return.

Four battalions came back to the United Kingdom sufficiently early to spend some time in England before travelling to the Midlands. The other seven came direct from the Empire to the Midlands, with four of them arriving at Avonmouth on 10th January, 1915, part of the same large convoy. The 2nd Battalion South Wales Borderers had the longest journey to make, in terms of distance. Stationed at Tientsin, in China, when war broke out, it had been involved in the action that led the capture of Tsingtao from the Germans in early November. During the fighting, the Battalion suffered 13 killed and 52 seriously wounded.

All the overseas units arrived safely, testimony to Britain's naval dominance at that time. However, according to the *Banbury Advertiser*, shortly before the departure from Avonmouth of the 4th Battalion Worcestershire Regiment, boulders were found strapped across the railway lines. The discovery was made by National Reservists on patrol duty and the signals were placed at danger until the boulders had been removed.[3]

The first battalion to return from the east was the 1st Battalion Royal Dublin Fusiliers, which had been stationed at Madras in August 1914. The process by which the Battalion made its way to the Midlands is well-documented and, although not entirely typical, can nonetheless serve as an example.[4] The other battalions are dealt with more briefly in the accompanying table.

The 1st Battalion Royal Dublin Fusiliers

As there were a considerable number of Germans and Austrians living at Madras, the Battalion's first duties, following the outbreak of war, involved safeguarding the water supply, oil tanks, public buildings and telephones. However, the oil tanks were set ablaze by the German cruiser *Emden*, which bombarded Madras on 22nd September. On 21st October, the Battalion orders announced that the Battalion was to hold itself in readiness to proceed to England at short notice. Families were not to accompany the Battalion. The orders of 31st October contained the names of 65 NCOs and men who were not to sail to England, either because of ill-health or because of their employment on other duties. However, when the Battalion finally left its headquarters at Fort St George, in Madras, on 13th November, a number of the sick had recovered sufficiently to travel. The Battalion's duties were initially handed over to the Madras Volunteer Guards, pending the arrival of the 1/4th Battalion of the Somerset Light Infantry, a Territorial unit.

The Battalion travelled by rail to Bombay, where it arrived on 16th November. Three days later, it embarked on the P and O steamer *Assaye*, part of a large convoy that increased still further in size when it was joined by other ships from Karachi on 21st November. In all, 32 ships made their way up the Red Sea and through the Suez Canal. Plymouth was reached on 21st December. The Battalion then entrained for Torquay, where the Dublins were billeted for three weeks, prior to their journey to the Midlands.

In their three-week stay in Torquay the Dublins evidently made many friends. They were billeted throughout the town and "such manly breezy fellows, full of their Indian stories and experiences, were received as welcome guests".[5] The soldiers were allowed a

The Returning Battalions: October 1914 – February 1915
(other than 1st Battalion Royal Dublin Fusiliers)

In addition to the 1st Battalion Royal Dublin Fusiliers, three other battalions returned to the United Kingdom sufficiently early to spend some time in England before travelling to the Midlands:

- **1st Battalion Essex Regiment:** in early November 1914, the half-battalion on Mauritius sailed for England. Upon arrival at Devonport, it was despatched to Warley Barracks, at Brentwood, in Essex, where the half-battalion from South Africa had already reported. On 14th December, the united 1st Battalion moved to Harwich before travelling on to Banbury on 18th January, 1915.
- **2nd Battalion Hampshire Regiment:** was directed to leave Mhow for Bombay on 31st August, although this was merely to replace another battalion that was returning to England. In the middle of November, the Battalion was relieved by the 7th Battalion Hampshire Regiment and was able to embark for England on 16th November, reaching Plymouth on 22nd December and travelling on to Romsey, in Hampshire. This allowed most men a short leave before the Battalion moved to Stratford-upon-Avon on 13th January.
- **1st Battalion King's Own Scottish Borderers:** sailed from Bombay on 2nd November and spent the period 17th November to 14th December in Egypt. The Battalion reached Plymouth on 28th December, went briefly to Warley Barracks in Essex and then travelled to Rugby on 19th January.

The remaining seven overseas battalions came direct from the Empire to the Midlands:

- **1st Battalion Border Regiment:** on 29th November, the 1st Battalion sailed from Burma for Calcutta in the 'P and O' Steamship *Novara*, disembarking after a four day voyage. On 5th December, it entrained for Bombay, which was reached on 9th December. Later the same day, the Battalion embarked on the *Corsican* and proceeded in a large convoy through the Suez Canal and Mediterranean to Gibraltar. Here it spent another five days, whilst transports arrived from China. The voyage home was then resumed and Avonmouth reached on 10th January. The Battalion proceeded at once by train to Rugby, where it arrived the next day.
- **1st Battalion Royal Munster Fusiliers:** began its journey from Burma to England on 21st October. A total of 19 officers and 879 other ranks proceeded initially to Calcutta, where they remained from 25th November to 4th December, before travelling by rail to Bombay. Here the Battalion embarked on the *Corsican*, on 9th December. On reaching Avonmouth on 10th January, an overnight train took the Battalion to Coventry on the 11th.
- **2nd Battalion Royal Fusiliers:** travelled in the same convoy from India as the RMF. On landing in England on 10th January, the Fusiliers travelled overnight from Avonmouth and arrived at Stockingford, near Nuneaton, on the morning of 11th January.
- **1st Battalion Royal Inniskilling Fusiliers:** left Secunderabad in India on 7th December, although a party of 10 N.C.O.s had been sent back to England in October to act as instructors for the New Army. The main party arrived at Avonmouth on 10th January before reaching Rugby on the 11th.
- **1st Battalion Lancashire Fusiliers:** left India for Aden in October, before sailing for England on 17th November. It reached Avonmouth on 10th January before travelling to Nuneaton on 12th January.
- **2nd Battalion South Wales Borderers:** had the longest journey to make. After its involvement at Tsingtao, in China, the Battalion moved to Hong Kong, before sailing for England on 4th December. It arrived at Plymouth on 12th January and Coventry on 13th January.
- **4th Battalion Worcestershire Regiment:** the last battalion that made up the 29th Division to be recalled. Withdrawn from Burma, it only arrived at Avonmouth on 1st February, 1915, before travelling on to Banbury on 2nd February.

short furlough, in small parties at a time. On 7th January, in anticipation of a further move, Lieutenant-Colonel Rooth handed over the Battalion Colours to the safe keeping of the Mayor of Torquay, expressing the hope that "some day some of us may come back ... to claim these Colours at your hands".[6] The final order to depart came at short notice, throwing out arrangements for a send-off dinner. However, on Sunday evening, 10th January, the Regimental band was still able to give a concert in the Torquay Pavilion, in aid of the town's hospitals. The occasion afforded the Mayor the opportunity to express the town's regret at the departure of the Fusiliers. The tobacco boxes, bearing the borough arms, the Battalion name and the date, which were to have been given to each man, had to be sent on after their departure. A small advance party from the Battalion left Torquay in the mid-morning of Sunday, 10th January, although the main body did not leave until the early hours of Tuesday, 12th January.

11. *The colours of the 1st Battalion Royal Dublin Fusiliers being handed over to the safe custody of the Mayor of Torquay; 7th January, 1915; Lieutenant-Colonel R.A. Rooth in front.*
(© Royal Dublin Fusiliers Association)

Shortly after 11 p.m. on 11th January, the buglers sounded the fall-in in various parts of the town. A misty rain was falling as the Dublins made their way to the Recreation Ground. The pickets were out and directed those who had "imbibed too deeply" to the assembly point, which soon became a scene of "noisy pandemonium", as civilians mingled with the soldiers. The Battalion then marched in companies to the station, in some cases with the soldiers' kit being carried by the friends they had made in the town. These friends included not just "young ladies" but also "a great many elderly matrons". More crowds waited at the station. Helpers handed each man a substantial pasty, there being no rations available on the journey. Two trains, leaving at 1.10 a.m. and 1.45 a.m. on Tuesday, 12th January, then conveyed the Battalion to the Midlands. As the trains pulled out of the town, a crowd on the Chelston railway bridge cheered the Fusiliers on their way.[7] The Dublins arrived in Nuneaton some 7 hours later.

∽

[1]   The full story of the time the 1st Battalion Border Regiment spent overseas before the Great War is told in "Glory Is No Compensation", although the main emphasis of the book is on the Battalion's experiences at Gallipoli. Ralph May with Stuart Eastwood and Clive Elderton: "Glory Is No Compensation"; Silver Link Publishing Ltd, 2003

[2]   *Coventry* Herald, 15th January, 1915; *Nuneaton Observer*, 15th January, 1915; *Leamington Courier*, 12th February, 1915

[3]   *Banbury Advertiser*, 4th February, 1915

[4]   Colonel H.C. Wylly: "Neill's 'Blue Caps', Vol. 3, 1914-1922"; Gale & Polden Ltd, 1923

[5]   *The Torquay Times*, quoted in the *Nuneaton Observer*, 22nd January, 1915

[6]   Colonel H.C. Wylly: op cit

[7]   *The Torquay Times*, as above

4

Billeting

ॐ

The billeting area

It was understandable that the billeting area would be described by Stair Gillon as "the very heart of Old England", with the rustic images that the phrase conveys.[1] In fact, it was a diverse area, in which rural communities and their market towns were juxtaposed with a major coalfield and attendant mining communities, a spa town and, notably in Coventry, some of the most technologically advanced manufacturing firms in the United Kingdom, which were already responding to the demands of the war with energy and purpose.

The area was quick to appreciate the potential advantages of billeting. In early December, Banbury Tradesmen's Association had written to Lord Kitchener extolling the virtues of the town as a billeting centre. These included an excellent rifle range and undulating countryside that would be suitable for training. The Association anticipated no difficulty arising from billeting but were keen to draw attention to the adverse impact on local trade that had resulted from the town's loyal response to the recruiting campaign and the enlistment of 2,000 local men. The Rugby Urban District Council also lobbied to secure the billeting of soldiers in the town.

Although both Banbury and Rugby would receive their share of billeted soldiers, the Army turned first to Leamington: enquiries were made, in the first week of December 1914, as to the suitability of the town for the billeting of some of the Divisional artillery. The artillerymen began to arrive in Leamington later that month. By the beginning of 1915, reports were becoming widespread that large numbers of troops were to be billeted in the Warwickshire area. The *Stratford Herald*, for example, was informing its readers on 1st January that it had heard "on excellent authority" that a battalion of regular soldiers was to be billeted on Stratford-upon-Avon within the next fortnight. A week later, it was reporting that military officials from Salisbury Plain were in the Warwickshire area making enquiries. Similar reports were soon circulating in the other major conurbations.

The billeting of soldiers in the area was unusual, although the sight of men in uniform would have been far more common than is the case today. The Royal Warwickshire Regiment had barracks at Budbrooke, near Warwick, and there were drill halls and other facilities in the main towns for the local units of the Territorial Force that had been established in 1908. In 1911, two companies of the 2nd Battalion Royal Munster Fusiliers had been billeted in Coventry during the national railway strike, although they appear to have been accommodated in licensed premises and not in civilian houses. According to the *Coventry Graphic*, the word 'billet' had become almost obsolete by 1915 and the paper reproduced a billeting order from 1873 to help prove its point.[2] In smaller communities, the process might be even more distant. The *Warwick Advertiser* reported that it was "close upon 90 years" since soldiers had been billeted in Long Itchington,[3] while the Royal Dublin

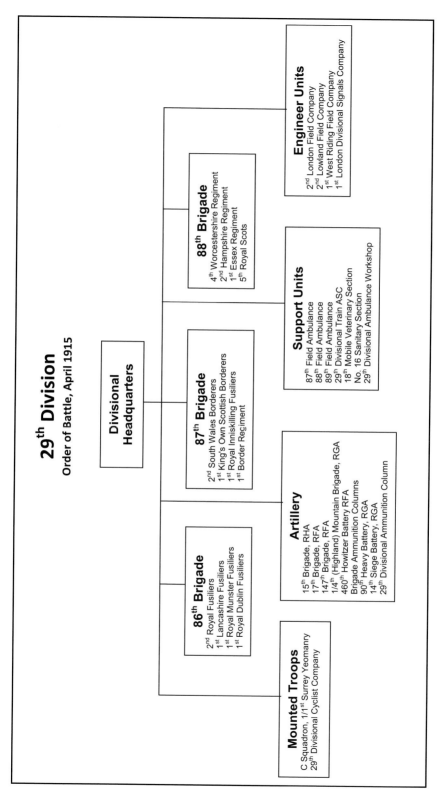

29th Division
Order of Battle, April 1915

Divisional Headquarters

86th Brigade
2nd Royal Fusiliers
1st Lancashire Fusiliers
1st Royal Munster Fusiliers
1st Royal Dublin Fusiliers

87th Brigade
2nd South Wales Borderers
1st King's Own Scottish Borderers
1st Royal Inniskilling Fusiliers
1st Border Regiment

88th Brigade
4th Worcestershire Regiment
2nd Hampshire Regiment
1st Essex Regiment
5th Royal Scots

Mounted Troops
C Squadron, 1/1st Surrey Yeomanry
29th Divisional Cyclist Company

Artillery
15th Brigade, RHA
17th Brigade, RFA
147th Brigade, RFA
1/4th (Highland) Mountain Brigade, RGA
460th Howitzer Battery RFA
Brigade Ammunition Columns
90th Heavy Battery, RGA
14th Siege Battery, RGA
29th Divisional Ammunition Column

Support Units
87th Field Ambulance
88th Field Ambulance
89th Field Ambulance
29th Divisional Train ASC
18th Mobile Veterinary Section
No. 16 Sanitary Section
29th Divisional Ambulance Workshop

Engineer Units
2nd London Field Company
2nd Lowland Field Company
1st West Riding Field Company
1st London Divisional Signals Company

Fusiliers, who arrived in Kenilworth in March, were "the first and only regular regiment to have stayed [in the town] within living knowledge".[4] (However, Kenilworth had been hosting four companies of the ASC since late January.) The lack of familiarity with the billeting process could work in both ways. The *Rugby Advertiser* noted that the battalions arriving in the town in January had "never been billeted on a population before".[5]

The billeting process

Public houses and hotels were still used to accommodate some members of the 29th Division, especially the officers. In Rugby, for example, most officers were given accommodation in one of Rugby's hotels, either the Royal George or the Three Horse Shoes or the Grand, although one officer resided in each section of the town in which men were billeted. However, in Nuneaton, officers were "taken to the residences of different gentlemen in the town". Battalion headquarters were located in suitable public buildings. In Nuneaton, for example, headquarters for the Royal Dublin Fusiliers were established at the Congregational Lecture Hall, for the Lancashire Fusiliers at the Peoples' Hall, Abbey Street, and for the Royal Fusiliers at the Stockingford Conservative Club, with Coton Road Lecture Hall, the Co-operative Hall and the Drill Hall being used for the regiments' stores.[6]

Some NCOs and men were also accommodated in public houses, invariably provoking criticism from householders who felt that they had been denied the opportunity to provide billets, as well as others who thought it put temptation in the way of the soldiers. In Stratford, for example, public houses and hotels were used to take some of the soldiers, overlooking the claims of "many private persons who would have been only too glad to entertain the good lads of Hampshire".[7] In Leamington, public houses, as well as empty properties, were used to accommodate a proportion of the soldiers in the town. For the most part, however, billets were found in private houses.

Communities were usually given one or two weeks notice of the arrival of the soldiers and accommodation had to be found in that time. Representatives of the military visited the communities chosen and worked with the local council and police to identify suitable properties. The Army had the right to enforce billeting, although such coercion was usually unnecessary, as local people generally responded very positively to the invitation to provide accommodation.

There was some variation in the approach adopted by the civil authorities. In Coventry, for example, offers to accommodate soldiers were invited from residents and the potential supply exceeded the demand. In Nuneaton, by contrast, the police appear to have applied a measure of pressure on households, leading the *Nuneaton Observer* to comment that not everyone wanted or needed soldiers and that a better approach would have been to advertise for applications to be sent to the local police, thereby helping those who needed the income.[8]

Banbury can be used to illustrate the process by which billets were found.

Banbury

On Friday, 8th January, the Mayor of Banbury was officially notified that the first contingent of troops to be billeted in the town (the 1st Battalion Essex Regiment) would arrive on Monday, 18th January. It would consist of 28 officers and 870 men. On 11th January, Captain Costeker, subsequently Brigade-Major to the 88th Infantry Brigade, came to make arrangements with the Billet Master, Chief Constable Wilson, and to inspect the billets. The town was divided into three areas and Army billeting forms were served upon the tenants of suitable houses. These forms required tenants to find quarters for a certain number of officers or men – usually between two and four per household. Householders who objected attended the Billet Master's office to give their reasons for so doing. In some cases these objections were upheld – especially if there was no male member of the household present – but, in general, they appear to have been overruled. The *Banbury*

Advertiser reported, with evident satisfaction, that "in the event of the excuses being frivolous … the number of men being billeted might be doubled".[9] However, it does not appear to have been too difficult for the authorities to find the required accommodation. Two days before the arrival of the 1st Battalion Essex Regiment, a small advance party from the Battalion, consisting of an officer and about a dozen NCOs and men, came to Banbury to inspect the billets before the soldiers went into them.

The billeting allowance

A billeting allowance was, of course, paid, with 17s 6d per week being received by a household for each soldier billeted upon it. The allowance was calculated on the basis of 9d a night for a bed and 1s 9d a day for food. Officers were billeted at 3s a night but would have been expected to pay separately for their food.[*] One contemporary estimate suggested that, once expenses had been met, the arrangement would leave a household with a surplus of about 5s a week for each soldier it had taken.[10] The allowance represented a considerable financial incentive for many households, especially those that had lost lodgers who had joined the armed forces. In the words of the war diary of the 86th Brigade Headquarters: "The inhabitants found the [billeting] rate remunerative and were anxious to take troops."[11] However, patriotism also played a part; no doubt this was especially so in households with family members who had also enlisted. In fact, the supply of potential accommodation exceeded demand. In Rugby, for example, the number of responses was so great that a waiting list was created in case further troops arrived.

Those not selected

Complaints invariably came from those who had not been selected for billeting, rather than from those who had. Bedworth appears to have been considered, although the town's case was probably not helped by Dr Orton, the local Medical Officer of Health, who felt that Bedworth was not a proper place to billet some 2,000 troops, fearing that it would result in overcrowding.[12] Others were less pessimistic and the authorities received offers of accommodation for 1,000, which it was felt would be a more realistic figure. In the event, none of the 29th Division came to town, leaving many to feel that Bedworth had been left 'in the cold', with one 'Tradesman' wanting the matter to be taken up by the local MP.[13] Although Nuneaton and Stockingford took more than 3,000 troops, some local residents were still left disappointed. In a letter to the *Nuneaton Observer*, a resident from Attleborough (a part of the town) wanted to know why, in particular, Gadsby Street had not been allowed to billet soldiers. "It has been spread about that the people are too low and degraded. … I think it is casting a nasty slur on respectable people."[14] In Rugby, it was felt that the claims of New Bilton had been overlooked and a 'New Biltonian' complained to the editor of the *Rugby Advertiser* that billeting would have helped offset the loss of men who had joined the Army.[15] (New Bilton did briefly receive men from the 29th Division, when the South Wales Borderers were moved there from Coventry in early March.)

Warwick also missed out, at least on the initial allocation of troops, although the town did take two infantry battalions in early March, when the Division was concentrated. This omission may seem surprising, given the numbers billeted in nearby Leamington, as well as Warwick's military associations. Whether the proximity of Budbrooke Barracks actually counted against the town is not known but there was subsequently a suggestion

---

[*] Whilst some observers considered the billeting allowance generous, it was pointed out that householders in Aldershot received £1 3s 7 ½ d per soldier per week. Indeed, the latter was the obligatory statute rate but Southern Command put pressure on those making the billeting arrangements to get the lower rate of 17s 6d accepted. It was subsequently discovered that the higher rate could be claimed but it is not known how many householders in the Warwickshire area may have done so. (War Diary of the Division's Administrative Staff; National Archives WO 95/4306)

made that "there were many people in Warwick not prepared at a moment's notice to accommodate men". When the Essex and Hampshire Regiments moved to Warwick in March, it was not for much more than a week and some local people were left out of pocket, having gone to the expense of buying bedsteads and bedding.[16]

It was also reported that many people in Solihull were in favour of billeting: trade had slumped during the winter months, with an increase in the cost of living and the absence of many young men who had joined the forces. People who obtained a living by letting had been particularly hard hit, as had been licensed victuallers.[17] Similar arguments were put forward by people living in Henley-in-Arden.

Last minute changes
Inevitably, last minute changes were made to arrangements. Rugby was initially told to expect about 1,600 men from the 1st Battalion Lancashire Fusiliers and the 2nd Battalion Royal Fusiliers. In the event, these battalions were sent to Nuneaton and to Stockingford, and Rugby had to find accommodation for three different battalions. At Kineton, the officials were told to expect 250 soldiers on Monday, 25th January, only for a message to come through at midday to say that they would not be arriving. However, nearly that number came to the town on 6th February. There was also some degree of adjustment after the initial billeting allocations had been made. Following the arrival of the Surrey Yeomanry in Stratford, on 23rd January, the *Stratford Herald* reported that a "few miserly hostesses" were punished by having the men withdrawn from the billets, whilst emphasising that the great majority of soldiers were almost unanimous in their praise of the accommodation provided. The *Midland Counties Tribune* reported a story, perhaps apocryphal, of the owners of a house in Nuneaton returning from holiday to find, to their surprise, two soldiers ensconced before the fire and smoking, "as if the house belonged to them". The maid servant was held culpable but she insisted that a policeman had appeared with a blue form and instructions to provide accommodation for two soldiers. It turned out that the correct billet was the same numbered house in a nearby road, to which the soldiers cheerfully departed.[18]

Not all of the Division was billeted in the Warwickshire area, or only arrived towards the very end of the billeting period:

- The 5th Royal Scots only travelled from Edinburgh to the area on 10th/11th March, staying in Leamington for just over a week.
- 'L' Battery of the 15th Brigade, Royal Horse Artillery, had already fought in France and was re-formed at St John's Wood after the losses it had suffered in the action at Néry, 1st September, 1914, during the retreat from Mons. It subsequently went from London to Avonmouth for embarkation.
- The 460th Howitzer Brigade, Royal Field Artillery, was formed at Stowmarket and was allotted to the Division on 1st February, 1915. However, it remained in Suffolk and travelled direct from Stowmarket to Avonmouth for embarkation.
- The Royal Garrison Artillery units: the 90th Heavy Brigade, the 14th Siege Battery and the 1/4th Highland Mountain Brigade were only attached to the 29th Division on 10th March and also joined the Division at Avonmouth.
- The 2nd London Company of the Royal Engineers was mobilised at Crowborough, in Sussex, and went directly to Avonmouth.
- The Divisional Ammunition Column was billeted in Slough until early March, when it moved to Taunton and from there to embarkation at Avonmouth.
- The Motor Ambulance Workshop was not billeted in the Midlands, although information on its location has not been found.
- No. 16 Sanitary Section was stationed the Duke of York's School, Essex, and from there to Avonmouth.

Overall, the billeting arrangements were remarkably successful. Within a short space of time, suitable accommodation was found for large numbers of soldiers, who were then quickly assimilated into the local communities. This success reflects not so much the legal powers at the disposal of the authorities but rather more the economic imperatives of the time, as well as a widespread determination to help the war effort. It may also signify an increasing ability on the part of British people to adapt to circumstances that were being changed by the war.

ᚼ

[1]   Captain Stair Gillon: "The Story of the 29th Division"; Thomas Nelson and Sons Ltd, 1925
[2]   *Coventry Graphic*, 26th February, 1915
[3]   *Warwick Advertiser*, 13th March, 1915
[4]   *Warwick Advertiser*, 13th March, 1915
[5]   *Rugby Advertiser*, 12th January, 1915
[6]   *Nuneaton Chronicle*, 15th January, 1915 and *Midland Counties Tribune*, 12th January, 1915
[7]   Letter in the *Stratford Herald*, 22nd January, 1915
[8]   *Nuneaton Observer*, 15th January, 1915
[9]   *Banbury Advertiser*, 14th January, 1915
[10]   *Nuneaton Observer*, 12th February, 1915
[11]   War Diary of the 86th Infantry Brigade Headquarters; National Archives WO 95/4310
[12]   *Coventry Herald*, 1st/2nd January, 1915
[13]   Letter to *Nuneaton Observer*, 15th January, 1915
[14]   *Nuneaton Observer*, 15th January, 1915
[15]   *Rugby Advertiser*, 13th February, 1915
[16]   *Warwick Advertiser*, 13th November, 1915
[17]   *Stratford Herald*, 19th February, 1915
[18]   *Midland Counties Tribune*, 15th January, 1915

12. *Royal Field Artillery in Greatheed Street, Leamington; December 1914.* (© Leamington Spa Art Gallery and Museum)

5

The Arrival of the Troops

cʒ

Of those who would subsequently make up the 29th Division, the first troops to come to the area were probably members of the 17th Brigade of the Royal Field Artillery. They began to arrive at Leamington on Friday, 18th December, travelling from Winchester, where they had been under canvas for a month since returning from India. The initial contingent of two batteries (the 26th and 92nd) comprised 5 officers, 350 men and 200 horses. Further batteries arrived in the last week of December and in the first week of January.

The arrival of the infantry battalions and support troops began in early January, with several thousand men flooding into the area in short space of time. Coventry has been chosen to illustrate the scenes that were repeated throughout the area in the early part of 1915.

13. *Royal Field Artillerymen in Leamington.* (© Paul Waller)

Coventry

The first soldiers to come to the city were from the 88th (1st East Anglian) Field Ambulance, a Territorial unit from the Royal Army Medical Corps. On Friday, 8th January, Captain Cogan arrived with an advance party and began preparing billets and stabling for the main party. On Saturday afternoon, he found that this would arrive the following day. It was made up of 10 officers and 236 men, accompanied by 30 horses and a large quantity of ambulance equipment, field tents etc. By the time it arrived, billets had already been identified, although stabling proved more difficult to find and it was necessary to go as far as Keresley before all the animals were housed. The problem for the RAMC was that the two infantry battalions due to arrive had already engaged practically all the available stabling in the city, in view of the possible allocation of 68 horses per battalion. The main party of the RAMC arrived at Coventry Station at 1.30 p.m. on Sunday (10th January), having travelled from Bury St Edmunds. They were met by Deputy Chief Constable Imber, along with a number of other police officers and a large party of special constables. The men were guided to their billets, which were mainly in Gulson Road, Payne's Lane and in the Stoke part of the city. However, those in charge of the horses were accommodated in the Radford district. An orderly room was established in an unoccupied factory. The billeting of the men had been completed by 3.30 p.m., although baggage and equipment had been left at the railway station for transportation on the Monday.

The infantry battalions arrived soon afterwards. An advance party of the 1st Battalion Royal Munster Fusiliers came to the city in the early hours of Monday, 11th January, to be followed, at about 9 a.m., by the first main party of 11 officers and 430 men, with 20 tons of baggage, and then, less than two hours later, by a second party of 10 officers and 445 men, along with 18 tons of baggage. Headed by the Regimental band, each group was marched to an assembly point: at Pool Meadow and Queen's Road, respectively. Billeting

14. *Members of the 88th (1st East Anglian) Field Ambulance in Coventry.* (© Phil Heffer)

arrangements had already been made by the Chief Constable, and Special Constables quickly escorted the men to their new homes, which were in the Earlsdon district and in the neighbourhoods of the Butts, Coundon Road and Pool Meadow. Soldiers were billeted street by street, until there were no more to be disposed of. It is not recorded how the houses were identified during this operation, although one practice was for the number of soldiers to be accommodated in a house to be chalked up by the side of the door. The soldiers would, no doubt, have sorted out among themselves the comrades with whom they wished to share. In the event, more billets were available in the designated areas than there were soldiers and some disappointment was expressed among those who had offered accommodation that was not used. Most of the officers were accommodated at the King's Head Hotel.

Less than 48 hours later, at 5 a.m. on Wednesday, 13th January, the first of three trains carrying the 1st Battalion South Wales Borderers arrived in Coventry. Again, the soldiers were met at the railway station by Superintendent Imber, accompanied by a number of the city police and a body of Special Constables, and they were taken quickly to billets in the Cheylesmore, All Saints, St Mary's and Stoke wards of the city. The first two trains had brought 22 officers and 785 men; a later train brought another 107 men, as well as the Battalion's baggage.

Thus, in the space of four days, more than 2,000 soldiers had arrived in Coventry and had been quickly housed. It was important that the billeting arrangements worked smoothly. The men were understandably tired after long sea voyages and, arriving directly from the Empire, clearly needed time to adapt to the much colder weather in England in January. When the Munster Fusiliers came to Coventry, they were still clad in their lightweight tropical uniforms, including shorts. The weather was a bitterly cold and many did not possess a greatcoat.[1]

15. *Members of the 1st Battalion Royal Munster Fusiliers shortly after their arrival in Coventry, January 1915.* (© Coventry History Centre)

Similar scenes were enacted elsewhere. Two battalions arrived in Rugby on Monday, 11th January, three battalions in Nuneaton and Stockingford between the 10th and 12th January, and one in Stratford on the 13th. In total, eight infantry battalions, as well as some of the support troops had been brought into the area. At the start of the following week, two more battalions arrived, at Banbury and Rugby respectively. Inevitably, the pace slowed thereafter but the process continued until the middle of February.

The Territorials

Predictably, it was the seasoned regulars from overseas who cut a dash and attracted the attention of the local newspapers. However, the less heralded arrival of some of the Territorial units also had its impact upon local communities – the numbers of soldiers being significant for some of the smaller towns and villages upon whom many were billeted. Kenilworth, for example, took four companies of the Army Service Corps that made up the Divisional Train. The town did not learn of their impending arrival from Dorset until the evening of Wednesday, 27th January, when the police began to make billeting arrangements. A few ASC men actually arrived on that Wednesday night, followed by another small party the following morning. Throughout Thursday, Inspector Parkinson and Sergeant Pink were visiting householders to see how many soldiers could be accommodated. The main contingent – about 250 men – arrived about 4 p.m. on Thursday, 28th January. The remaining contingents came during the first week of February, by the end of which some 400 men were billeted in the town. The ASC's wagons arrived on Wednesday, 3rd February, their horses having been brought from Leamington on the preceding Sunday and placed in stables throughout Kenilworth.[2]

On Saturday, 6th February, the main body of the 1st West Riding Field Company of the Royal Engineers came to Kineton in two special trains. A small advance party had arrived the previous day. The Company totalled 7 officers and 232 soldiers and were generally billeted in private houses.[3] Similar numbers of men found a temporary home in Southam, when the 2nd Lowland Field Company of the Royal Engineers arrived from Scotland on the morning of Monday, 15th February.

A warm welcome

Whatever the reservations some may have held about the impact of so many soldiers on local communities, the welcome extended to the soldiers was always a warm one. In Nuneaton, even the advance party of the Royal Dublin Fusiliers, consisting only of an officer and a dozen men, was met by a large crowd that had gathered at the station. They, and the others who followed, were provided with warm cocoa, mince pies and cakes by Mrs Cole; these were understandably appreciated.[4] When the main body of the 2nd Battalion Hampshire Regiment arrived in Stratford-upon-Avon, large crowds had assembled in the vicinity of the Great Western Railway Station to greet them. The Mayor led an official deputation and other dignitaries included the Rev. Canon Melville, in uniform as chaplain to the Warwickshire Royal Horse Artillery. As the soldiers marched through the town, they were "warmly greeted" by the residents. Light refreshments were served to them at the Corn Exchange, before the men made their way to their billets.[5] In Banbury, the first trainload of soldiers from the 1st Battalion Essex Regiment was played into the town by a band from a Territorial unit. Flags were hung out and a large crowd welcomed the troops as they marched to the Horse Fair. Boy Scouts assisted the police in showing the men to their billets.[6]

The troops' presence immediately transformed the towns in which they were staying. With the arrival of the Hampshire Regiment, Stratford in the evening "seemed alive with pedestrian traffic". "Khaki Coventry – Where Are The Civilians?" was the caption of a photograph in the *Coventry Graphic*,[7] whilst Nuneaton soon became "a town of khaki" and "a military depot".[8]

The Arrival of the Division in the Billeting Area: Main Dates

Friday, 18th December: 17th Brigade Royal Field Artillery began to arrive at Leamington from Winchester. The initial contingent of two batteries (the 26th and 92nd) was made up of 5 officers, 350 men and 200 horses. Further batteries arrived in the last week of December and in the first week of January.

Friday, 8th January: Captain Cogan and an advanced party of the 88th (1st East Anglian) Field Ambulance, RAMC, arrived at Coventry.

Sunday, 10th January: the main party of the 88th Field Ambulance arrived at Coventry from Bury St Edmunds. During the evening, an advance party of the Royal Dublin Fusiliers arrived at Nuneaton.

Monday, 11th January: the advance party of the 1st Battalion Royal Munster Fusiliers arrived in Coventry in the early hours, followed by two trainloads of men and equipment at about 9 a.m. and 11 a.m. The 2nd Battalion Royal Fusiliers reached Stockingford, having travelled overnight from Avonmoth. The soldiers came in two special trains, one arriving at Stockingford at 7.40 a.m. and the other at 8.40. Between 9 and 11 a.m., the 1st Battalion Royal Inniskilling Fusiliers and the 1st Battalion Border Regiment arrived in Rugby, also travelling directly from Avonmouth.

Tuesday, 12th January: the 1st Battalion Royal Dublin Fusiliers and the 1st Battalion Lancashire Fusiliers arrived in Nuneaton. The Dublins, who had left Torquay late on Monday, arrived between 8 and 9 a.m. and the Lancashires between 10 and 11 a.m.

Wednesday, 13th January: the first of three trains carrying the 1st Battalion South Wales Borderers from Devonport arrived in Coventry at about 5 a.m. In the afternoon, the main body of the 2nd Battalion Hampshire Regiment arrived in Stratford-upon-Avon.

Monday, 18th January: two trains carrying the 1st Battalion Essex Regiment arrived in Banbury from Harwich during the afternoon.

Tuesday, 19th January: the 1st Battalion King's Own Scottish Borderers arrived in Rugby from Warley, followed by the arrival of the 87th (1st West Lancashire) Field Ambulance, RAMC.

Saturday, 23rd January: 'C' Squadron of the Surrey Yeomanry arrived in Stratford-upon-Avon and the 89th (1st Highland) Field Ambulance, RAMC, arrived in Nuneaton. The RAMC had been transferred from Bedford, where they had been stationed since the end of January, having moved there from Aberdeen. 5 officers, 170 NCOs and men, and 88 horses of the Divisional Signal Engineers (1st London) came to Leamington.

Thursday, 28th January: the main body of the Divisional Train (Wessex), which consisted of 246, 247, 248 and 249 Companies of the Army Service Corps arrived in Kenilworth from Dorset, where they had been for about three months.

Tuesday, 2nd February: the 4th Battalion Worcestershire Regiment arrived in two trains and was billeted at the Grimsbury end of Banbury.

Friday, 5th February: 18th Mobile Veterinary Section arrived at Leamington from Fareham and was billeted at Whitnash.

Saturday, 6th February: the main body of the 1st West Riding Field Company of the Royal Engineers arrived in Kineton by two special trains. A small advance party had arrived the previous day.

Monday, 15th February: the 2nd Lowland Field Company of the Royal Engineers arrived in Southam from Scotland.

Thursday, 11th March: the 5th Battalion Royal Scots arrived in Leamington from Edinburgh.

Although details appear not to have been given in the local newspapers, subsequent references suggest that the Brigade Ammunition Columns were also present in Leamington.

16. *The main party of the 2nd Battalion Hampshire Regiment arriving in Stratford, 13th January, 1915.*
(© Shakespeare Birthplace Trust)

The soldiers generally appear to have reacted favourably both to their billets and to the warmth of the welcome they received from the local population. Some of the Territorials, like those who went to Kineton, had been living for several months under canvas before their arrival in the Midlands. For some members of the 87th Field Ambulance, which had moved in October 1914 from the Liverpool area down to Kent, accommodation had included tents and then empty houses in Sevenoaks, a chandler's shop in Charing and a "dirty empty house in Canterbury" that was "swarming with lice", as its occupants discovered the next morning "and for many days after".[9]

Most of the regulars had never been billeted upon a civilian population before. Bandsman H. Brown, of the 1st Battalion Lancashire Fusiliers, said of his billets: "beautiful house and kind people", whom he was soon calling "Ma and Pa".[10] Billeted men in Rugby were quoted as being amazed "at the heartiness of the welcome". "We never experienced so much kindness before. People seem to be competing with each other to make us welcome, and the experience is very different from what we have been accustomed to."[11] Of course, local newspapers were always keen to point out examples that showed their locality in a favourable light and that bolstered wartime morale but there are plenty of other instances that could be cited to support the idea of a mutual regard between the soldiers and civilian population being quickly established.

അ

[1]   *Coventry Herald*, 15th/16th January, 1915
[2]   *Coventry Herald*, 5th/6th February, 1915
[3]   *Rugby Advertiser*, 13th February, 1915
[4]   *Nuneaton Observer*, 15th January, 1915
[5]   *Stratford Herald*, 15th January, 1915
[6]   *Banbury Guardian*, 21st March, 1915
[7]   *Coventry Graphic*, 22nd January, 1915
[8]   *Nuneaton Observer*, 15th January, 1915
[9]   Young, W. Alfred: diary; Liddle Collection, Leeds University Library, GALL 116
[10] Brown, H.: diary; Liddle Collection, Leeds University Library, GALL 015
[11] *Rugby Advertiser*, 23rd January, 1915

17. *Royal Munster Fusiliers setting potatoes. The soldier on the right is apparently knitting.* (© Coventry Graphic)

18 & 19. *South Wales Borderers in domestic mood.*
(© Coventry Graphic)

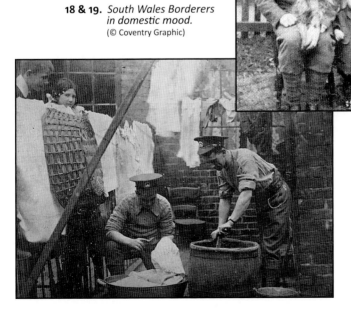

6

Settling in

ೞ

The soldiers adapted quickly to their new surroundings. After a good meal, the Munster Fusiliers and the South Wales Borderers were soon out and about exploring Coventry. The Munsters "were to be met in twos and threes in every highway and byway. ... Talkative and curious, but invariably courteous, it did not take Coventry folk many hours to form a great liking for these sunburnt Irishmen, even those whose exuberance and conduct on the first day were just a little pronounced."[1] The South Wales Borderers also "wasted little time in making themselves acquainted with their temporary home".[2] Some of the Borderers had relatives in Coventry and had visited the city before. Youngsters were quickly captivated by the soldiers in the city and were soon following them around. As elsewhere, buttons and coins were given away as souvenirs to the soldiers' admirers. In Rugby, Scouts patrolled the town during the first few evenings after the troops' arrival, to help show the soldiers to their billets or to the recreation rooms established for their use. "If you want to know the time", said one Border Regiment officer, "ask a Scout".[3]

There were, of course, some problems. The attraction of the public houses was strong, especially for soldiers arriving from abroad after long sea voyages (see Section 10). Inevitably, there were also some unsatisfactory billets (again, see Section 10) but these appear to have been the exceptions to the rule. Nor were the guests always amenable, at least at first: the *Midland Counties Tribune* for 15th January claimed that many of the landladies in Nuneaton were having "a rough time". Overall, however, the arrangements worked well, no doubt helped by the generous billeting allowance, but also by the natural hospitality of local people. There were also a few organisational problems to resolve. On Wednesday, 13th January, the Munster Fusiliers reassembled on Pool Meadow in Coventry. In the course of their travels, many of the rifles had got into the wrong hands and some men even ended up with two. A parade was called to put matters right and the proceedings were watched by a large crowd.

In general, the appearance and behaviour of the soldiers quickly reassured: "a fine stalwart lot of fellows" was the opinion of the *Rugby Advertiser*. Many were still wearing their Indian sun helmets.[4] The *Coventry Herald* was soon noting the popularity of the Munsters and South Wales Borderers, who had been useful in the houses, making their own beds, washing up, cleaning grates, and so on. In the Grimsbury area of Banbury, an officer and seven men of Worcestershire Regiment were praised for their prompt action in extinguishing a chimney fire. The owner of the house was particularly appreciative, as the fire might easily have spread. The soldiers turned out with such alacrity that the fire had been extinguished by the time the Banbury Fire Brigade arrived.[5] There was obviously an element of wartime propaganda in such reports, as there was in many of the photographs of soldiers that appeared in the newspapers.

20. *Royal Munster Fusiliers sorting out rifles; Pool Meadow, Coventry, 13th January, 1915.* (© Coventry History Centre)

Leave

The warmth of the welcome may have offered some compensation for the shortness of home leave that the soldiers were granted. Traditionally, men returning from a long spell of service overseas were entitled to a lengthy spell of leave. According to the *Rugby Advertiser*, men of the 1st Battalion Border Regiment, after eight years service abroad, would be given about six months furlough but they now had to content themselves with four days. The Battalion was divided into two halves for this purpose, the second group going on leave after the first had returned.[6] Other regiments appear to have made similar arrangements. Officers fared rather better in terms of leave and some officers, certainly senior ones, brought their families to the billeting area.

Bandsman H. Brown of the 1st Battalion Lancashire Fusiliers enjoyed a furlough of five days in late January. He travelled up to Manchester by train from Nuneaton and spent a busy and enjoyable time catching up with his family and friends, as well as with Pollie, who would appear to have been his girl friend or fiancée. His stay coincided with Pollie's 21st birthday. Among other activities, he was able to watch Manchester City defeat Bolton Wanderers 2:1 and, on the final day, he made a will. By 27th January, he had returned to Nuneaton and was back in "the same old routine" of route marches and other training. A month later he had a weekend pass and again returned home. Leaving Manchester at midnight on Sunday, he was back at Nuneaton at 6.30 a.m. on Monday, 1st March, and on parade two hours later. "Felt tired before the day was out."[7]

Relatives sometimes visited. One glimpse of this, albeit an unhappy one, was an accident on the evening of 27th January, in New Bridge Street, Nuneaton, when Instructor A. Hutchinson, 6th Battalion Lancashire Fusiliers, was struck by a motor van whilst visiting his son, Private Charles Hutchinson, of the 1st Battalion Royal Dublin Fusiliers. The father, who had travelled down from Southport, was taken to hospital suffering from severe bruising; his son, who was walking with him, was unharmed.[8] Of the units billeted in the area, the soldiers of the 4th Battalion Worcestershire Regiment were invariably the ones closest to their relatives.

21. *A soldiers' club in Coventry.* (© Coventry Graphic)

Soldiers' clubs

Local communities certainly did not stint themselves in their efforts to make the newly-arrived soldiers feel at home. This stemmed partly from a concern that the soldiers might prove a nuisance if left to their own devices, but patriotism and community pride also played their part. Local committees were quickly formed to provide recreational clubs and 'entertainments'. In Rugby, nine premises had been identified even before the first soldiers arrived in the town, of which at least five were opened on 12th January, the day after the arrival of the first two battalions; the other places were held in reserve. These clubs were organised by a central committee.[9] In Stratford, the arrangements linked the Companies of the 2nd Battalion Hampshire Regiment to specific venues: 'A' Company in the Wesley Hall, 'B' in the Parish Parlour, and so on. In Nuneaton, the initiative was taken by the local churches, with a meeting convened at the Old Grammar School on 8th January, in advance of the soldiers' arrival. Both the Church of England and the Nonconformist bodies were represented and the meeting was chaired by Canon Deed. A representative of the YMCA was also present. The discussion focused on whether it was better to have a central venue or to allow individual organisations to make their own arrangements. In the end, it was decided to obtain St George's Hall as a central venue but to proceed with other recreation rooms as well.

Throughout the billeting area, assembly rooms, village and church halls, clubs, school rooms and the like were made available and furnished with additional chairs and tables, as well as pianos, gramophones, billiard tables and other games. Writing materials were provided, along with books, newspapers and periodicals; arrangements were usually made for soldiers to purchase cigarettes and non-alcoholic refreshments at cost price. In many cases, individuals loaned furniture and other equipment, or agreed to pay for the cost of items such as newspapers. Otherwise, expenses were borne by the local communities, with funds established to which local people were invited to contribute. Further money was raised through concerts, the sale of refreshments etc. At the rooms in Nuneaton, expenditure took the form of lighting, heating, cleaning, the purchase of food and drink, printing, stationery, furnishings and rent, although the latter was waived in the case of some of the clubs in the billeting area. When the rooms were closed in March, following the departure of the troops, the Nuneaton committee found itself with a modest balance of £7 (retained in case other troops were billeted in the town); in Rugby, there was a debt of £20 and an appeal was made for assistance.[10]

Some recreation rooms, such as those in schools, could only be opened to the soldiers in the evening; others were open all day. For the most part, those who ran the committees and organised rooms and functions came from the local communities, often drawing on the experience of those traditionally involved in charitable work. Women probably featured more strongly than men. As was to be expected, the YMCA was heavily involved. The Association already had over 600 centres in the country, including those in Coventry and Leamington. In anticipation of the arrival of the 29th Division's soldiers, the YMCA initially proposed erecting a marquee on Greyfriars Green in Coventry. However, this idea was dropped and, instead, the YMCA adapted its property in the Quadrant, extending the facilities that had for some time been made available for all soldiers in the city. The YMCA was also involved in assisting a number of the local committees in the billeting area. In Nuneaton, for example, they undertook the supervision of the facilities at St George's Hall, as well as helping to defray some of the expenses of the other main recreation rooms.

The popularity of the soldiers' clubs seems to have varied. In early February, Oswin Creighton noted in his diary that the club at Stockingford was being closed, as it was not being used, the men apparently being content with the comforts of their billets. However, the *Leamington Courier* reported that the YMCA rooms in the town "were being used by hundreds of soldiers daily" and that a privately run club at Milverton was also proving very popular. One difference may have been that a smaller proportion of soldiers were billeted in people's homes in Leamington – the club at Milverton being located in an area where more than 100 men were staying in empty houses. A local lady, Mrs W.B. Jones, had decided that they would appreciate some 'home comforts' and a house, 'Guy's Dale' was found. Others rallied round with gifts and a comfortable club was established. It was open from 10 a.m. to 10 p.m. to all soldiers in the town and a husband and wife were found to live there and undertake domestic duties. Refreshments, at a minimal charge, were available through the day. Ladies assisted during the afternoon at 'tea hour' and two gentlemen in the evening, the latter also "helping out with songs". The club was popular: on Sunday, 10th January, for example, 170 men "availed themselves of the Club's shelter".[11]

Entertainments

Concerts, including smoking concerts, musical evenings, dances, whist drives, billiard matches and the like were also quickly arranged and continued throughout the time that the troops were in the area. Quite what the soldiers really made of the pianoforte duets, recitations, impersonations, violinists, ventriloquists, conjurers and the like is not recorded. Officially, they were always "most appreciative" and, in practice, they may well have been – the garrison life from which they had returned was often far from exciting. The fact that the *Warwick Advertiser* for 20th February could express disappointment at an attendance of 150 for an entertainment in Kenilworth – and that "the fourth of the week" – suggests that the audiences must often have been very good indeed.[12] However, the *Banbury Guardian* was to conclude that "if anything the hospitality was somewhat overdone, as the men preferred a more free and easy time when off duty".[13]

The soldiers themselves frequently contributed to the entertainments. Take, for example, the whist drive organised at the Union Club in Stratford, on Wednesday, 24th February, in aid of funds for the General Hospital. The Surrey Yeomanry were well-represented and troopers played their part in making the evening a success, with "delightful vocal and instrumental items in the interval", a couple of recitations, "which afforded immense amusement", and some "excellent rag-time songs".[14]

Local churches were quick to welcome soldiers to their services and also organised concerts and other entertainments for them. In February, for example, a Soldiers' Plum Pudding Night was organised at the Friends Meeting House in Rugby by the Fellowship Relief Committee. The idea was to make up for the Christmas meal that had been missed by the troops when they were sailing back. About 200 soldiers attended.

22. *Soldiers from the Hampshire Regiment studying a bulletin, produced by the Official Press Service, in a shop window in Stratford.* (© Shakespeare Birthplace Trust)

Other organisations, such as the Good Templars, were happy to offer their facilities. The Sir Thomas White's Lodge in Coventry gave up one of its usual meetings in February to allow the Royal Munster Fusiliers' Pride Lodge to meet, elect their officers and transact their business.[15] The Swanswell Lodge of the Ancient Order of Buffaloes also welcomed the soldiers in Coventry, organising a series of concerts for them. The Irish Club in Coventry was quick to extend a welcome to the Munster Fusiliers. In Kenilworth, the local lodge of the Druids entertained NCOs and men at the Virgin's Inn. The Rugby Conservative Club organised concerts and billiard matches, and the local Co-operative Society musical evenings and whist drives. Not to be outdone, the pupils of St Matthew's School in Rugby revived their successful entertainment of the previous November for the benefit of the soldiers.

In the larger towns, the soldiers also had access to a wide variety of cinemas, music halls and theatres, which must have been a novelty for many of them after years overseas. In Coventry, one soldier told a local journalist that it was the first time he had been to a theatre in 14 years: "all we get in Burma is Boy Scout pictures".[16] Amongst the entertainments on offer to soldiers in Nuneaton, in early February, were: 'The Mystery of the Bank Vault', as well as war pictures, at The Palace; Mr A.E. Bintio, the miniature comedian, at The Royal; 'Babes in the Wood' at The Grand Theatre; and the "great drama" 'Harbour Lights' at The Picturedrome, with the prospect of Woodward and Page, "the well-known trick cyclists and instrumentalists" to top the following week's programme. If the soldiers favoured entertainment with a war theme, then Coventry could offer: 'The Slackers' (The Hippodrome), 'Soldiers of Fortune' (The Empire) and 'A Belgian Girl's Honour' (The Globe).[17] The management of the Picture House in Stratford decided to run two shows nightly to cater for the large numbers of soldiers in the town.

The soldiers' welfare

More mundane than some of the entertainments, though no doubt equally welcome to the soldiers, were the comforts offered by the Nuneaton Slipper Baths. The Baths Committee decided to reduce the admission to 1d for men in uniform and the baths were soon enjoying the patronage of nearly 80 soldiers a day. By the end of January, more than 1,000 soldiers had made use of the baths. Not unreasonably, this prompted the local newspaper to wonder how many more civilians might use the baths if the tariff were permanently set at 1d.[18] Admission to the swimming baths in Rugby was also available to soldiers for 1d, though the second class baths (3d) and slipper baths (6d) were more expensive. The decision was taken not to admit the public when the baths were being used by the soldiers, although this was not because of the soldiers' behaviour, which was described as "excellent" and reflecting great credit on their regiments.[19] In April, it was announced that upwards of 1,000 free treatments for rheumatism, sciatica and the like had been given at the Spa Baths to soldiers in Leamington, especially to the officers and men of the Worcestershire Regiment during their short stay in the town in March.[20]

Fresh uniforms seem to have been issued quickly, if this had not been done prior to arrival. The soldiers of the Border Regiment, for example, were still wearing their lightweight, khaki drill uniform when they reached England. The men were marched through a large shed at Avonmouth, which acted as a clothing depot, and received winter underclothes and serge uniforms.[21] The Lancashire Fusiliers were issued with khaki uniforms on 11th January, while still on board their transport ship, the *SS Grantully Castle*, which was then anchored at Avonmouth.[22] Nonetheless, there were appeals made in Leamington for warm clothing for the artillerymen billeted there. Although local people were being thanked in early January for their gifts, the appeals were repeated, with the Commanding Officer of the 17th Brigade Ammunition Column asking, in early February, for flannel shirts, balaclava helmets, vests, socks, gloves and mittens for his men, or for the money with which to procure these items. He pointed out that the unit had only been in existence for a very short time and lacked funds.[23]

The military authorities had, of course, insisted in advance on suitable hospitals being available in the billeting area and these were kept quite busy during the time the Division was in the area (see Section 12). To take one example: in Rugby, 'Ashlawn', a substantial residence in Hillmorton Road, was made available by its owner for use as a Red Cross Hospital for soldiers. It was equipped with 27 beds, most of the furniture being loaned by local residents. The Hospital was run by the Hillmorton and Dunchurch Voluntary Aid Detachments and furniture to equip it was lent by local people. By the time the troops left, just over 100 cases had been dealt with at the Hospital, with more than 90% of the patients discharged for duty.[24]

❧

1   *Coventry Herald,* 15th/16th January, 1915
2   *Coventry Herald,* 15th/16th January, 1915
3   *Rugby Advertiser,* 16th January, 1915
4   *Rugby Advertiser,* 16th January, 1915
5   *Banbury Guardian* and *Banbury Advertiser,* 18th February, 1915
6   *Rugby Advertiser,* 16th January, 1915
7   Brown, H.: diary; Liddle Collection, Leeds University Library, GALL 015
8   *Nuneaton Observer,* 29th January, 1915
9   *Rugby Advertiser,* 9th and 16th January, 1915
10 *Nuneaton Observer,* 26th March, 1915; *Rugby Advertiser,* 27th March, 1915
11 *Leamington Courier,* 15th January, 1915
12 *Warwick Advertiser,* 20th February, 1915
13 *Banbury Guardian,* 11th March, 1915
14 *Stratford Herald,* 26th February, 1915
15 *Coventry Herald,* 19th/20th February, 1915
16 *Coventry Herald,* 15th/16th January, 1915
17 *Coventry Herald,* 26th/27th February, 1915
18 *Nuneaton Observer,* 29th January, 1915
19 *Rugby Advertiser,* 23rd January, 1915
20 *Leamington Courier,* 16th April, 1915
21 Ralph May with Stuart Eastwood and Clive Elderton: "Glory Is No Compensation"; Silver Link Publishing Ltd, 2003
22 Brown, H.: op cit
23 *Leamington Courier,* 5th February, 1915
24 *Rugby Advertiser,* 20th March, 1915

7

Building a Division

cs

The composition of the Division

The first day of mobilisation for the 29th Division was Monday, 18th January, and Divisional Headquarters were established in the Manor House Hotel, in Leamington. The man appointed to command the new division was Major-General Frederick Charles Shaw. As a Brigadier-General, he had commanded the 9th Brigade during the early stages of the war. Sir John French said that Shaw had shown "great dash" and had performed "magnificent work" during some of the hardest fighting. Wounded on 12th November, 1914, when a shell hit his headquarters during the First Battle of Ypres, Shaw was at home recuperating when he was given his new command. He proved to be popular and competent, although he was not destined to command the Division on active service. His principal staff officer on the operations' side (G.S.O.1), Colonel O.C. Wolley-Dod, took up his position on 20th January. The arrival of brigade commanding officers soon followed: on 24th January, Brigadier-General W. R. Marshall to 87th Brigade; on 27th January, Brigadier-General H.E. Napier to 88th Brigade and, on 1st February, Brigadier-General S.W. Hare to 86th Brigade. On 14th February, Brigadier-General R.W. Breeks was appointed to command the Divisional Artillery.

23. *The Manor House Hotel, Leamington Spa, used as the Headquarters of the 29th Division.* (© John Fortnum)

As was the practice at the time, the 29th Division had three infantry brigades of four battalions each (see the diagram on Page 30). For obvious reasons, the 86th Brigade was a 'Fusilier Brigade'. The mix of English, Scottish, Welsh and Irish battalions meant that the 87th Brigade became known as the 'Union Brigade'. The 88th Brigade enjoyed no equivalent moniker. Brigade headquarters were in Nuneaton, Rugby and Stratford-upon-Avon respectively. As noted, the Royal Scots joined the 88th Brigade after its concentration at Warwick and Leamington in early March. The 1st Battalion Middlesex Regiment had initially been identified as the 'last battalion'.[1] The 1st Middlesex had gone out to France in August 1914 and was attached to the 6th Division in October. Presumably, it would have transferred to the 29th Division had the Division gone first to France. The substitution of the 5th Battalion Royal Scots,[*] "an Edinburgh Territorial unit of good repute",[2] appears to coincide with the decision to send the 29th Division to Gallipoli. (However, other factors may have determined the decision.)

A division of the period was a largely self-contained military unit and infantry brigades were therefore accompanied by divisional artillery, engineers, mounted troops and other support units, including field ambulances, and members of the Army Service Corps. An Ordnance Depot was established at the Skating Rink in Leamington and the stables of the town's Regent Hotel were used as a Remount Depot. The allocation of the other units that made up the 29th Division in early 1915 is shown on the diagram on Page 30.

Although regarded as the last of Britain's regular army divisions to be created in the Great War, a number of units, in addition to the 5th Battalion Royal Scots, were drawn from the Territorial Force. These were 'C' Squadron of the Surrey Yeomanry; the 1/4th Highland Mountain Brigade, Royal Garrison Artillery; the three companies from the Army Service Corps, which made up the Divisional Train; the three field companies from the Royal Engineers; the Divisional Signal Company; and the 87th, 88th and 89th Field Ambulances.

Training begins

As soon as the Division's units were settled into billets, training got under way. Large scale manoeuvres at brigade or divisional level were constrained by the nature of the local countryside, with its small, enclosed fields, and by the widespread dispersal of the billets. Indeed, Major T.H.C. Frankland, Brigade-Major of the 86th Infantry Brigade, felt that:

> "under the system of billeting with subsistence, men have been very well fed, and are very fit. On the other hand billets are very scattered and for training purposes and for discipline the system is extremely inconvenient. It takes a long time to collect men and is difficult to turn out at short notice."[3]

Nonetheless, training at company and battalion level could proceed. The first soldiers to commence training belonged to the artillery units that had begun to take up billets in Leamington in December 1914. In her diary for 28th December, Cordelia Leigh recorded how Colonel E.P. Smith had approached her brother, Dudley, Lord Leigh, for permission to use the Deer Park at Stoneleigh Abbey for artillery practice.[4] On 1st January, two Army aeroplanes landed on the Shrubland Hall estate at Leamington. The subsequent flights over the town attracted considerable interest. It was understood that the purpose of the visit was to train with the RFA and RHA batteries quartered in Leamington in observation work.[5] On 11th January, Cordelia Leigh reported that:

---

[*] The title 5th Royal Scots has been used rather than 1/5th Royal Scots in accordance with the Divisional and Regimental histories and Major A.F. Becke's Order of Battle of Divisions – on the grounds that the second line unit (the 2/5th Battalion) did not go on active service.

24. *Divisional artillery in training, at what seems to be Stoneleigh Deer Park; December 1914.*
(© Warwickshire County Record Office and R.L. Graham Studio)

"Col. Smith brought some of his Field Artillery for practice in the Deer Park; they had no real ammunition, but practised directing their cannon on a mark – a certain tree on the top of a ridge; they practised near the large gate leading from the Stare Bridge road into the Park. An officer from Head Quarters came to inspect while we were there. Rupert's little boy, "Robin", aged 6, was an interested observer, and attached himself to Col. Smith with whom he has made great friends!"

On the 27th January, Cordelia recorded:

"It was interesting to see the trenches which the soldiers from Leamington had dug in the Deer Park. ... They came upon water in several places so that some trenches had water in the bottom. The guns were covered over with bracken and branches of larch to conceal them from imaginary airships overhead. They dug about 8 small trenches. School children from Stoneleigh and Ashow were brought over by the teachers to see the sight."[6]

Route marches

Given that most of the Division's soldiers were trained professionals, much of the emphasis was placed on route marches, to restore levels of fitness that had been reduced during long sea voyages. Both the Royal Dublin Fusiliers and the Lancashire Fusiliers undertook route marches from Nuneaton the day after their arrival, as did the Hampshire Regiment at Stratford. The Dublin Fusiliers and the Hampshire Regiment had been back in England for some time; however, the Lancashire Fusiliers had only disembarked at Avonmouth on the previous day. Within four days of their arrival, route marches were also being undertaken by the three battalions at Rugby, who had also travelled to the Midlands direct from Avonmouth.

25. *Troops from the 29th Division on a route march near Coventry, accompanied by wagons and field kitchens; late February or early March, 1915.* (© Coventry Graphic)

Battalions were preceded, during the day at least, by their regimental bands, and the marches quickly became a popular spectacle in the area, with people lining the streets of the towns and villages to watch the soldiers go by. In Coventry, as elsewhere, the marching powers of the soldiers were much admired: "they swing along with an ease and elasticity".[7] This interest extended to the other units. On 22nd February, the 1st West Riding Field Company passed through Honington in full marching order, with horses, wagons and cycle corps. Their arrival drew a large number of spectators from the neighbourhood, "who evinced great interest in the military visitors".[8] Route marches also gave the opportunity for the Division's transport to be tested, along with other equipment, such as travelling field kitchens.

The m.G.o - decidedly annoyed

26. *Members of the 1st Battalion King's Own Scottish Borderers passing through Bilton; "the M.G.O. [Machine Gun Officer] decidedly annoyed" seems to be the comment.* (© Warwickshire Library and Information Service)

Once these excursions became commonplace, it was the events that were out of the ordinary that subsequently attracted newspaper attention. Thus the *Nuneaton Observer* (12th February) reported an incident at Wolvey where the officer in charge of one of the battalions stationed in the town was asked by an old lady for the men to stop in front of her cottage so that she could present each man with an apple. The lady's request was acceded to, "much to her gratification". The same edition of the *Observer* also reported a route march by the Royal Dublin Fusiliers, which included a halt at the factory of Messrs Atkins Bros in Hinckley, at which each man was presented with a pair of khaki mittens. The factory was temporarily closed, so that its employees could welcome the 'Tommies', "there being much fraternising between the soldiers and the 'lassies'". The Regimental bands played popular music and "the drums were rolled in stirring fashion". Army songs were sung and the participants in the scene spent a memorable time. After 30 minutes, the Fusiliers gave three rousing cheers for the firm and continued on their way. The Battalion's smart military appearance was much admired: as they marched over the crest of the hill in Bridge Street, "crowds of female admirers" broke into the ranks and shook hands with the soldiers. On Watling Street, near Higham, the progress of the Dublins was also watched by the 29th Division's GOC, Major-General F.C. Shaw.

Fitness training could be quite intense. During February, for example, the 2nd Battalion Royal Fusiliers took part in 12 route marches, including two Brigade marches. No fewer than 8 of these took place in the first two weeks of the month. These were interspersed with drill parades and some work of a more practical kind, such as practising attacks or occupying trenches by day and by night. A nearby rifle range was used on two occasions.[9] However, it may have been the case that the Territorial units, which had previously been based in the UK, were not worked as hard. The ASC troops at Kenilworth were involved in drills, a matter of considerable interest to the townspeople, but it was also reported that the men had finished their hard training by the end of January and would be kept on light work "until they are sent to France".[10]

Some of the route marches took place in the dark. Local people were warned, for example, about troops marching between 5 and 10 p.m. within a 6 mile radius of Coventry. They were advised that troops would always be on the proper side of the road, preceded by a man with a white flag and followed by a man carrying a red light. Warnings were also issued, to motorists and others, not to try to break through the ranks of marching troops. One pedestrian who did so in Nuneaton received something of a surprise. As the Dublin Fusiliers were returning from church parade on 17th January, a young "knut" (a fashionable young man) walked through between the Regimental band and the officer commanding; he was promptly deposited the other side of a fence. The local paper thought that this treatment was "richly deserved" and felt that "there is a young man in Nuneaton who will never break through the ranks of marching soldiers again". What adds flavour to the story is that it was the officer in command who despatched the miscreant![11]

Other training

In addition to route marches, there were company exercises and shooting practice and soldiers also undertook trench digging, some of it at night. Local newspapers took the opportunity to photograph machine-gun crews using their weapons "under modern conditions", and signallers with their flags. Engineers billeted at Kineton practised bridge construction at the lake at Compton Verney and a Divisional bomb-making and explosives 'school' was established near Rugby. The officers who attended the 'school' could practise their newly developed skills on bits of railway line, trenches and wire entanglements. Lieutenant Guy Nightingale, of the 1st Battalion Royal Munster Fusiliers, who journeyed from Coventry to attend a course, found it all "very dangerous" and throwing grenades at night "more dangerous still". He seemed quite relieved that only one casualty was sustained on the course he attended; this was an officer from the Royal Inniskilling Fusiliers.[12]

27. *Members of the 2ⁿᵈ Battalion Hampshire Regiment digging trenches – and playing to the camera; near Stratford.* (© Shakespeare Birthplace Trust)

Training at brigade level

Over time, the battalions began to come together to work in larger formations. The *Midland Counties Tribune* for 12ᵗʰ February reported that the 86ᵗʰ Brigade's first route march had taken place that morning, although it appears not to have involved the Royal Munster Fusiliers, who were billeted in Coventry. The three Nuneaton based battalions assembled on their parade grounds before setting off; as the oldest regiment, the Royal Fusiliers led the way. Marching from Stockingford, they were met at the top of the Wharfe Hill by the Lancashire Fusiliers, followed by the Royal Dublin Fusiliers, again reflecting precedence. Huge crowds watched their progress out of Nuneaton, local factories temporarily shutting to allow their workers to witness the event. The Royal Fusiliers were preceded by their band, which was followed by the cycle corps, officers and rank and file, along with their fifes and drums. Transport included ammunition and baggage wagons, and field kitchens. Although the Lancashire Fusiliers were not accompanied by their transport, they had "a splendid lot of horses, all finely groomed and looking spic and span". Their drums and fifes came first, with the brass instruments in the middle of the battalion. The Dublins reflected the Royal Fusiliers in their accompanying equipment and the three battalions were followed by a field ambulance, "an object of much interest". The men "looked in splendid trim" and their officers rode back and forth to inspect the line. The march continued through Bedworth and Bulkington to the crossroads a mile to the north of Wolvey; the return journey was by way of Attleborough. In all, "the spectacle presented was a dazzling one".

Brigade exercises were only undertaken at the end of the billeting period. The 87ᵗʰ Brigade held an exercise on 4ᵗʰ March, at Bilton Grange, and, on 11ᵗʰ March, the 86ᵗʰ Brigade staged a mock battle, on the banks of the River Avon at Stoneleigh. However, the exercise was curtailed because of the Division's inspection the following day.

Routine work: the 87ᵗʰ Field Ambulance

The war diaries for the units that made up the Division generally started with the departure of these units overseas, or were only perfunctory for the period in England. One exception was the 87ᵗʰ Field Ambulance of the RAMC, for which a detailed diary for March 1915 was kept. A Territorial unit (originally the 1ˢᵗ West Lancashire Field Ambulance), which was

28. *Royal Munster Fusiliers taking part in a relaxed firing practice; near Coventry, March 1915.* (© Coventry Graphic)

29. *Royal Munster Fusiliers with machine guns, near Coventry, March 1915: "a warlike scene in a quiet Warwickshire lane" was the caption to this photograph from the* Coventry Graphic. (© Coventry Graphic)

30. *King's Own Scottish Borderers training at Bawnmore House, near Rugby.* (© Warwickshire Library and Information Service)

mobilised in the Divisional area, its diary provides an insight into the work being carried out during its stay in Rugby. Each day, apart from Sunday, began early for the men, with a parade at 7.15 a.m., followed by a second parade at 9.30 a.m. Mornings were usually occupied with drill or short route marches, or with practices, such as packing the unit's wagons. Afternoons might be given over to lectures. Equipment had to be overhauled and consignments of blankets, saddlery, harnesses etc had to be assimilated. In the middle of the month, 73 mules were received. Fresh details of men from the Reserve were taken onto the strength, in order to replace those deemed unfit for overseas service. At the 87th Brigade's exercise on 4th March, the unit practised establishing and equipping a dressing station and collecting wounded by night. The local Voluntary Aid Detachment (VAD) Hospital served as a Casualty Clearing Station (CCS) and the chain of treatment, with the evacuation of the wounded, was completed by using borrowed motor vehicles to take 'wounded' men from the CCS to rail heads at Rugby. For a while, the unit's officers also took medical charge of the VAD Hospital at Ashlawn, although it is not clear whether this was done primarily to improve medical care at the Hospital or to give the officers relevant experience.[13]

One member of the 87th Field Ambulance was Private H. Harris. He later recalled how conscious the RAMC men were of the presence of the regular soldiers in the town and how careful they were to ensure that their conduct and military bearing did not fall short of the standards set by the regulars. As "mere Territorials", they were "very impressed – nay overawed – by the discipline and smartness of the regular soldiers". Perceptively, he noted that, although the regular officers and men "were always correct in their approach to each other, the men saluting smartly when an officer approached, their relationship seemed to be one of loyalty and friendliness", based, as it was, on long service in the Empire.[14]

31. *No. 3 Section of the Divisional Signal Company in Leamington, February 1915; Captain R.C. Freeman seated in the centre.* (© Leeds University Library)

The strengthening of the Division

The 29th Division was also re-equipped, although the Division had to wait until the requirements of the 28th Division had been met for anything other than clothing.[15] Thereafter, the situation began to improve. In February, for example, the 2nd Battalion Royal Fusiliers received a steady flow of new equipment, including water carts, g.s. (general service) wagons, two machine guns, new boots, rifles, entrenching tools and two field kitchens. Seventeen heavy draught horses were attached to the Battalion and six drivers transferred from the ASC to manage them.[16] As new equipment arrived, it was tested out. On 17th February, the Dublin Fusiliers practised with their new rifles at the Kingsbury Rifle Range. They travelled by train from Nuneaton, in two parties, and fired 10 rounds per man, despite adverse weather conditions. Rain fell continuously and the mud and surface water made it seem "like being in the trenches". The Royal Fusiliers and Lancashire Fusiliers also put in time at Kingsbury.[17]

Battalions and other units were brought up to strength. Thus, the 2nd Battalion Hampshire Regiment acquired 181 NCOs and men from the Regiment's 3rd (Reserve) Battalion on 31st January.[18] The following day, 1st February, the Royal Fusiliers received a draft of 81 men from Dover; on 2nd February, the 1st Battalion Royal Munster Fusiliers a draft of 127 men; and so on. Following medical inspections, those deemed unfit for overseas service were sent back to join the reserve battalions or to regimental depots: thus 15 Royal Fusiliers were sent to Dover on 9th February. On 19th February, 11 boys from the Battalion, who were deemed too young, were sent to the depot at Hounslow.[19] On 16th February, the 1st Battalion Royal Dublin Fusiliers despatched "39 men, immature soldiers and temporarily unfit" to the Regiment's 3rd Battalion in Cork.[20] In addition, a small number of officers left following their promotion, usually for service in France.

There were also movements within the Division. These included the formation of the 29th Divisional Cyclist Company. This was some 200 strong, to which the 1st Battalion King's Own Scottish Borderers contributed one officer and 17 NCOs and men, the 1st Battalion Royal Munster Fusiliers one officer and one NCO and 11 men, and so on.[†]

Young officers who joined the Division included 2nd Lieutenant Charles Palmer, who had been gazetted in December 1914, and who joined the 1st Battalion Royal Inniskilling Fusiliers. He is pictured on Page 58, involved in what appears to be a planning exercise with fellow officers from the 87th Brigade and, it would seem, at least one officer from the 86th Brigade. It was not always easy for the newcomers to integrate with seasoned regulars. 2nd Lieutenant R.B. Gillett, who had been commissioned into the Hampshire Regiment in August 1914, was ordered to join the 2nd Battalion in Stratford in February. He later said of his experiences:

> "I felt completely out of my depth ... a young officer with no experience whatsoever, very little training as most of my time had been spent drilling recruits. I had no real field practice and only one field day and there I was landed with a Battalion of hardened regulars. ... I felt completely inadequate and I had a major battle with my Company Commander. ... The training was for me appalling. We never did less than a 16 mile route march a day or a day in the country on extra field work. The training ground on that occasion was some 5 or 6 miles away. So we had to march out that distance. A long day in the field and march back again, all in full marching order, and I found that a great trial."[21]

[†] At Gallipoli, the Cyclist Company found itself used for guard duties and a variety of manual jobs, such as constructing roads.

32. *2nd Lieutenant Charles Palmer, 1st Royal Inniskilling Fusiliers (third from left) and officers from the 1st King's Own Scottish Borderers and 2nd South Wales Borderers, 87th Brigade; unidentified planning exercise, probably late February / early March 1915. Officer second from left appears to be from 1st Battalion Lancashire Fusiliers, 86th Brigade.* (© Steve Jenkins)

Brigade inspections

As the time for departure approached, so the battalions and other units were brought together in their respective brigades, with each brigade managing at least one inspection. On 25th February, the three battalions of the 86th Brigade based in Nuneaton marched, via Attleborough and Wolvey, to a point near Shilton, where they were joined by the Royal Munster Fusiliers from Coventry. The combined Brigade was then inspected by Major-General Shaw. Rumours had circulated in the area that the King was to make the inspection and a great many people followed the soldiers in the hope of seeing their sovereign. They were to be disappointed in that respect but the spectacle of over 4,000 troops, along with transport, field kitchens etc was an impressive one and "Shilton had the day of its life".[22] Major-General Shaw must have had a busy day because he also inspected the 87th Brigade on 25th February. Given that the 86th Brigade was inspected in the morning, with the troops beginning their return march at about 11.15 a.m., it would seem likely that the inspection of the 87th Brigade took place in the afternoon, with Shaw conveyed by staff car from Shilton to the intersection of the Fosse Way and the London Road, near to Stretton on Dunsmore. Here he took up position "on the road side, with a triangular piece of greensward as the saluting base and the main road for a parade ground."[23] This was the spot at which the King would take the salute of the 29th Division on 12th March.

On 1st March, it was the turn of the 88th Brigade to assemble; they did so at Radway Grounds, beneath Edgehill, where the 2nd Battalion Hampshire Regiment from Stratford met the two battalions billeted at Banbury: 1st Battalion Essex Regiment and 4th Battalion Worcestershire Regiment. Here they were inspected by Brigadier-General Napier. Despite the cold March weather, with alternating showers of rain and sleet, the proceedings were also watched by a large number of local people.

An untested Division

The 29th Division was to leave the area without any proper training at brigade level and with none at divisional level. To make matters worse, no brigade or divisional training was possible after the Division landed in Egypt, as the troops were employed on fatigue duties. Indeed, Colonel Wolley-Dod subsequently made the point that the Division was not tested as such until the fighting of 28th April, 1915, given that the landings on 25th April were essentially fought at brigade and battalion level – and by the 28th April the Division was below half strength and inadequately supported by artillery. Fortunately, both morale and gallantry at the regimental level were high.[24]

℣

1   Captain Stair Gillon: "The Story of the 29th Division"; Thomas Nelson & Sons, 1925. The 1st Battalion Middlesex Regiment is also identified as being allocated to the 88th Infantry Brigade in the entry for 9th January, 1915, in the War Diary for the Brigade's Headquarters. The Middlesex Regiment's replacement by the 5th Royal Scots is recorded on the 8th March: National Archives WO 95/4312.

2   Captain Stair Gillon: op cit

3   War Diary of the 86th Infantry Brigade Headquarters; National Archives WO 95/4310

4   Sheila Woolf and Chris Holland: "A Strange Time: The Diary and Scrapbooks of Cordelia Leigh"; Warwickshire Great War Publications, 2012

5   *Warwick Advertiser*, 9th January, 1915

6   Sheila Woolf and Chris Holland: op cit

7   *Coventry Herald*, 15th/16th January, 1915

8   *Stratford Herald*, 26th February, 1915

9   War Diary of the 2nd Battalion Royal Fusiliers; National Archives WO 95/4310

10   *Leamington Courier*, 29th January, 1915

11   *Nuneaton Observer*, 22nd January, 1915

12   Guy Nightingale Papers: National Archives PRO 30/71; Diary January-December 1915, PRO 30/71/5

13   The War Diary of the 87th Field Ambulance Brigade, National Archives WO95/4309

14   Harris, H.: memoirs; Liddle Collection, Leeds University Library, GALL (REC) 161

15   War Diary of the 86th Infantry Brigade Headquarters; National Archives WO 95/4310

16   War Diary of the 2nd Battalion Royal Fusiliers; National Archives WO 95/4310

17   *Nuneaton Observer*, 19th February, 1915

18   *Stratford Herald*, 5th March, 1915

19   War Diary of the 2nd Battalion Royal Fusiliers; National Archives WO 95/4310

20   War Diary of the 1st Battalion Royal Dublin Fusiliers; National Archives WO 95/4310

21   Gillett, R.B.: transcript of interview with Peter Liddle, 1973; Liddle Collection, Leeds University Library, GS 0624

22   *Nuneaton Observer*, 27th February, 1915

23   *Leamington Courier*, 26th February, 1915

24   Captain Stair Gillon: op cit

8

The Soldiers and Local Communities

☙

The Division's economic impact

By the end of February, there were probably about 16,000 men from the 29th Division billeted in the area, with this number increasing by another 1,000 in early March, with the arrival of the 5th Battalion Royal Scots. As noted, one contemporary estimate was that, of the 17s 6d per week received by a household for each soldier billeted upon it, usually 12s would be spent on feeding the soldier.[1] This meant that, during the billeting period, perhaps £9,000 – £10,000 each week was going into the hands of local grocers, bakers, butchers, dairymen and the like. In Nuneaton, for example, the *Observer* estimated that 2,000 extra loaves were needed every day as a consequence of the presence of nearly 4,000 soldiers in the town. Presumably some of the modest profit made by households would also have passed directly into the local economy. Soldiers, of course, were not well paid but another contemporary estimate was that each was spending about 5s per week – collectively, about £4,000. This was principally to the benefit of local tobacconists, publicans and places of entertainment, though soldiers also appear to have bought a lot of sweets and fruit. On 15th January, the *Coventry Graphic* happily reported that the newly arrived soldiers, after such a long spell abroad, "are in a purchasing mood".

The Co-operative Society in Coventry was one retailer to notice the benefit of so many soldiers in the city. "I have never seen sales so big as they were last week", said Mr W. Jones, President of the local Society, in early February.[2] It was calculated that an extra £2,000 was being spent in Coventry each week and that the Society was receiving its share of that. The *Rugby Advertiser* subsequently claimed that an additional £8,000 per week had been put into circulation by the troops stationed in the town, although the figure seems on the high side.[3] Even the brief time, in early March, that the Royal Dublin Fusiliers were in Kenilworth brought a boost to local trade.[4]

The Division had other requirements, such as food consumed by soldiers during training, or fodder and stabling for more than 3,000 horses and mules. The demand for stabling was high: as already noted, the RAMC, arriving later in Coventry than the infantry, had to go as far as Keresley to complete the accommodation of its 36 horses. In Banbury, horses were stabled at licensed houses, with 18 at 'The Plough', 15 at 'The Flying Horse' and so on, while, in Stratford, the 100 horses of the Surrey Yeomanry were stabled at the larger houses and business premises in the town.

Although local people were discouraged from buying soldiers drinks, they were invited to purchase foodstuffs and gifts for their benefit. "Nuneatonians", for example, were urged to do their duty and "Feed our Gallant Soldiers on Matthews Sausages",[5] while another Nuneaton firm, "Hazelwood – Specialists in Soldiers' Necessaries", proclaimed

33. *Soldiers and children; Coventry, February 1915.* (© Coventry Graphic)

their wares under the heading "Presents for Soldiers". Their "useful and life-saving goods" included gloves and mittens, scarves, pants, vests, and khaki handkerchiefs. That they also offered for sale the badges of the regiments billeted in the town makes it clear that their intended market was specific rather than general, although many of the town's soldiers who were abroad or in training would also be recipients of local generosity.[6] In similar vein, Batt's Khaki Dept, in White Street, Coventry, advertised the badges of the Royal Munster Fusiliers and the South Wales Borderers; these cost 6d each.[7] As the time approached for the troops to leave Banbury, T.F. Baker, Tailor and Outfitter, thoughtfully reminded the townspeople of its many "Useful Presents for Soldiers and Sailors".[8] Tobacconists in Kenilworth had their stock almost entirely cleaned out as townspeople purchased gifts for the soldiers. On the eve of their departure, the men of the 2nd Battalion Hampshire Regiment were each given a briar pipe, inscribed "A Gift from Stratford-on-Avon", although where these were manufactured is not known.

As noted, communities that did not have troops billeted upon them often felt that they had missed out, whereas those which had been favoured were aware of their good fortune. Indeed, the *Nuneaton Observer* went so far as to proclaim that: "from an economic point of view, the billeting of soldiers has proved one of the finest happenings in the history of Nuneaton".[9] Following the departure of the 29th Division, hopes were expressed that troops might once again be billeted in the Warwickshire area and further billeting did take place, although not on the same scale; for example, Leamington hosted the 30th and 31st (Reserve) Battalions of the Royal Fusiliers between November 1915 and January 1916.

Sport

Traditionally, sport was an important part of regimental life and its contribution to the physical fitness of soldiers recognised by their senior officers. The arrival of the soldiers in the Warwickshire area temporarily revitalised sport, which had declined following the enlistment in the forces of so many local young men.

Several of the battalions had fine football teams, including the 2nd Battalion Royal Fusiliers, which had seven army internationals. These teams were soon playing against each other and also against local sides. The matches could attract considerable crowds: some 3,000 watched the South Wales Borderers play a team from the Humber Company, in Coventry; the game was held in benefit of the dependents of Private A. Townend, Royal Warwickshire Regiment, and a former employee of the firm, who had been killed in December 1914.[10] In Stratford, a record crowd of more than 1,000 watched a match at the Pearcecroft, on Saturday, 23rd January, between teams representing the town and the 2nd Battalion Hampshire Regiment. The Mayor kicked off. The soldiers won "a clean, well-fought match 3:1".[11]

In Rugby, the town's Football Club soon placed their ground at the disposal of the troops for football and other games, in response to a request from the military authorities.[12] Both the Royal Inniskilling Fusiliers and the King's Own Scottish Borderers were reported to have good Association football teams and the battalions entered teams for the annual Rugby Hospital Cup. On 31st January, the Border Regiment beat Rugby F.C. 5-1 in the first semi-final, the game being watched by 2,000 spectators. A few days later, in the second semi-final, the Royal Inniskilling Fusiliers defeated a K.O.S.B. team 4-0. When the Fusiliers went on to win the Hospital Cup, beating the Border Regiment 3-0, the game attracted between 2,000 and 3,000 people. Proceeds from the competition went to St Cross Hospital, to the local division of the St John's Ambulance Brigade and to the Rugby District Nursing Association. One of the battalion commanders presented the Cup and said that each of the 22 men who had played would receive a medal and that this would remind them all of their time in Rugby and of the friends they had made there.

On 4th February, the South Wales Borderers turned out at Highfield Road against the Bantams team of Coventry City FC. Despite the 'Citizens' including a number of amateurs and several members of the Coventry City Police, they secured a comfortable 2:0 victory. In mitigation, it was pointed out that the Borderers were out of practice and were not used to a grass pitch, having played on unturfed surfaces in India and China. The attendance on this occasion was small, with a sprinkling of soldiers, including some of the wounded soldiers recuperating at local hospitals. On 20th February, the Borderers enjoyed a measure of revenge, beating "an unfamiliar team representing Coventry City". The City team included a Belgian, Emile Steinon, in goal, who was "responsible for one or two good saves" but still conceded four goals.[13] On the same day, the 2nd Lowland Field Company of the Royal Engineers played Southam, the result being a, perhaps diplomatic, 5:5 draw.

There were also cross country, hockey and rugby matches. In Nuneaton, T. Belcher's XV played the Lancashire Fusiliers, on 20th February, "in the first and last game of the season". The local side, which included 12 players who had represented Nuneaton the previous season, enjoyed a comfortable victory by 25 pts to 3. The sun shone, the ground was in good condition and the game was enjoyed by "a capital ring of spectators".[14] Nor did the soldiers billeted in Rugby enjoy success in their games of Rugby football, with teams from each regiment being defeated by Rugby School, and the King's Own Scottish Borderers losing to a Rugby and District team.

Other sporting fixtures in Rugby included Rink hockey, in which roller skates were used, and boxing tournaments. On 9th February, a Grand Military Boxing Tournament was announced, to be held at the Rugby Rink on 11th and 12th February. Ticket prices ranged from 1s to 4s, with soldiers in uniform admitted to the 1s seats at half price. Proceeds went to the Belgian Relief Fund and the winners were presented with a silver cup, valued at £10 10s. In the event, the Tournament was won by the Border Regiment, helped by Drummer Crone, champion lightweight boxer of India. A seven round contest between Crone and Jim Smith of Rugby was won easily by Crone, "who was never really extended"; his opponent, by contrast, "went through the ropes on four occasions". St Matthew's Boys' School was one of the schools providing entertainment at the tournament, in the form of songs and dances. A second tournament was held in March.

Local rifle clubs were quick to challenge army teams to shooting competitions. A team from Coventry Chain defeated the regulars, though consolation for the soldiers may have been found in the post-match exercise drill performed by the Ladies of the Coventry Chain Athletic Club, "not the least interesting part of the proceedings", according to the *Coventry Graphic*.[15] Teams from the 2nd Battalion Hampshire Regiment were twice entertained by the One Elm Shooting Club: the first fixture ending in a tie, the second being won by the Club.

Not all of the intended sporting fixtures went to plan. In January, the famous Birchfield Harriers came to Rugby to run against a team of soldiers. Unfortunately, "none of the soldiers turned out, thus robbing the event of much of its interest". Several members of the British Thomson-Houston (B.T.H.) Harriers competed but "failed to make much of a show" on the 6 mile course, though the *Rugby Advertiser* did point out that very few runners were now left in the district, as practically all of them had joined up.[16] However, in early February, teams from the Border Regiment and Royal Inniskilling Fusiliers did take part in a cross country run, along with an VIII from Rugby School; the School emerged triumphant.

Among billiards matches was one in early February at Rugby Conservative Club, between members of the club and the soldiers from the King's Own Scottish Borderers. After the match, which was won by the townspeople, the soldiers were entertained to supper. In February, it was announced that all officers serving in His Majesty's Forces, and quartered in Warwickshire, had been elected honorary members of the Warwickshire County Golf Club.

Music

The battalions all had bands, as did some of the smaller units. Standards could be high and the bands appear to have been in demand. In Rugby, for example, the Border Regiment's band gave concerts on Sunday afternoons (and sometimes Wednesday afternoons) at Caldecott Park, listened to by several thousand people if the weather was good. The band also played at the Temple Speech Room and in the Great Hall of Rugby School, for the benefit of the pupils. In addition, Rugby School played host to the pipers of the King's Own Scottish Borderers. In Stockingford, the Royal Fusiliers organised a 'Military Soiree' at the Council Schools. Such occasions were often used to raise money for local causes. Thus, on 21st February, a military concert was held at the Picturedrome in Nuneaton in aid of the town's General Hospital. A large audience listened to the Regimental bands of the Royal Dublin Fusiliers and the pipe band of the Scottish Ambulance Corps, as well as civilian performers.

Predictably, the military bands were used to assist recruiting campaigns. On Sunday, 7th February, for example, the band of the Royal Dublin Fusiliers played at a "grand performance" at the Picturedrome, which included the patriotic film 'The British Army in Training'. It was hoped that the evening would stimulate recruiting and receipts went towards providing comforts for wounded soldiers in the town. The occasion was repeated the following Sunday, on this occasion the Dublin Fusiliers being supported by both the pipe band of the Scottish Ambulance Corps and by civilian performers. In early February, the band of the Royal Munster Fusiliers accompanied departing troops from the 7th Reserve Battalion of the Royal Warwickshire Regiment to Coventry railway station. On the whole, however, it appears that the presence of the soldiers and their bands did not have much effect upon recruitment in the area.

One exception, however, was John Loughan, from Coton Road, in Nuneaton. He was determined to join the Army, especially after the stay of the Royal Dublin Fusiliers, when he became "a regular associate of the Dublin boys". The fact that John had only celebrated his fourteenth birthday the previous September acted as no deterrent. At 5 feet 6 inches, and with "a muscular frame", he had no difficulty persuading the recruiting officer that he was 19 and he duly enlisted in the Royal Dublin Fusiliers. When his parents found out, they immediately took steps to secure his release. However, given his evident determination to re-enlist, if he was brought back home, they agreed to John becoming one of the band boys. By May, Private 'Jacky' Loughan was at Naas Depot, in County Kildare. John's grandfather and great-grandfather had both been soldiers and John had apparently exhausted all the military books in Nuneaton Library. The local newspaper, far

34. *The band of the 1ˢᵗ Battalion Royal Munster Fusiliers playing members of the 7ᵗʰ Reserve Battalion Royal Warwickshire Regiment to Coventry Station; 2ⁿᵈ February, 1915.* (© Coventry History Centre)

from condemning his enlistment, was glad to be able to publish "his stirring story", which, it was felt, had given "a noble lead" to all the single men in Nuneaton who had yet to enlist.[17]

In January, the band of the Royal Munster Fusiliers assisted at the funeral of Private Christopher Horsley, an 18 year old from Kenilworth, who died of pneumonia whilst still in training with the 7th Battalion Royal Warwickshire Regiment. Horsley was interred at Coventry Cemetery. In March, the band of the Royal Fusiliers was involved in the funeral at Stockingford of Private Joseph Clarke, 2nd Battalion Royal Warwickshire Regiment, who had been killed in an accident at Milverton Station, in Leamington. A few days later, the bugles, fifes and drums of the Royal Munster Fusiliers participated in the funeral at Coventry Cemetery of Driver Joseph Bourne, who had died at Portsmouth of a brain haemorrhage. The Fusiliers also provided a firing party.

At a more informal level, soldiers often contributed to the entertainments in the area. Their ranks contained a good many competent musicians and singers, as well as men adept at 'comic renderings', and they clearly entered into the spirit of the occasion, determined to reciprocate the hospitality being shown to them. In Rugby, members of the RAMC twice visited the town's Poor Law Institution to provide entertainment for the inmates. The instrumental selections, recitations and songs were well received.[18] Oswin Creighton recounted how he went in search of singers to accompany the band of the Royal Fusiliers at a concert that had been arranged in Nuneaton. At a local music hall, he enlisted "a coy and buxom woman who sang patriotic songs and … a blind man who played the concertina". Both proved very popular. Admittedly, the music hall lady "had no voice" but compensated "by boundless cheek and made the men sing choruses".[19]

35. *An impromptu group of musicians from the 2nd Lowland Field Company, Royal Engineers, outside the Dun Cow, Southam. The civilian on the front row is thought to be Ernie Owen, the pub landlord.*
(© Alan Griffin)

Church parade:

1st Battalion Royal Munster Fusiliers - Coventry - January 10th to March 16th 1915

36. *Sergeant Drummer Joseph Hickey at the head of the drummers of the 1ˢᵗ Battalion Munster Fusiliers in Hill Street, Coventry. In action, bandsmen acted as stretcher bearers.* (© Dr Tadhg Moloney)

37. *Members of the 1ˢᵗ Battalion Royal Munster Fusiliers lined up in Hill Street, Coventry, facing St Osburg's Church, prior to attending Sunday service.* (© Dr Tadhg Moloney)

Religion

The men's spiritual welfare was, of course, considered important and each Sunday began with church parade. Services for Anglicans, Catholics, Presbyterians, as well as members of other churches, such as Wesleyans, were held. The local interest in the soldiers was reflected in the large numbers of people who turned out to watch the troops march to and from the churches, led by their bands. The *Rugby Advertiser* reported "dense crowds" outside the Parish Church on 18th January and "several thousand" on the 25th. In Stratford, the centre of interest was the Hampshire Regiment, which paraded in the Rother Market before marching to the Parish Church, played there by the Battalion's fife and drums.[20] In Kineton, the spectacle of the church parade of the West Riding Company was considered a "very picturesque one … Perhaps nothing resembling it has been witnessed since the Battle of Edgehills."[21]

For many soldiers, of course, church parade was something that they had to accept, however unenthusiastically. Oswin Creighton, newly appointed Chaplain to the 86th Infantry Brigade said of his experiences with soldiers billeted in Nuneaton: "I find them very nice, very civil and easy to talk to. But I feel quite at sea as to how to do any direct religious work with them."[22] However, some were more devout and entered into the spiritual life of the local communities. One was Serjeant James Johnston, of the 1st Battalion Border Regiment. A 29 year-old regular soldier from Cumberland, he contacted the Rugby Baptist Church through the 'welcome club' at the Baptist Schoolroom. "He lived for spiritual things. … His faith was his dominant passion", said Pastor J.H. Lees. During his time in Rugby, Johnston gave talks at the Baptist Church, including one on astronomy and "quite the best missionary address we have ever had". He also conducted services at the Baptist Chapels at Dunchurch and Draycote, and at the Rugby Railway Mission. An enthusiastic advocate of temperance, he was reported as "having induced many men in the Regiment to sign the total abstinence pledge".[23] It seems that his wife, Mary, joined him at Rugby and participated in his religious work.[24]

Other soldiers contributed to sustaining the work of the Home Mission in Rugby. Sergeant Mudd, of the Royal Inniskilling Fusiliers, gave an address to the Mission's annual meeting, held at the Wesleyan Church in January. He explained the Christian work among soldiers in His Majesty's Army. Representatives of the Lodge of Good Templars, connected with the Royal Inniskilling Fusiliers, provided vocal accompaniment at the meeting, including a solo, "Our God is marching on", sung by Private Miller. The Military Good Templar Lodge held meetings at the Co-operative Hall during their stay in Rugby, including dances and concerts. Nor did the YMCA forget its task of catering for the moral and spiritual welfare of the men, as well as their physical comfort. It sought to use its Recreation Rooms to inculcate in soldiers "the habits of temperance, thrift and an aversion to gambling". The Association "wanted to make the soldiers better men and better Christians."[25]

☙

1   *Nuneaton Observer*, 12th February, 1915
2   *Coventry Herald*, 5th/6th February, 1915
3   *Rugby Advertiser*, 27th March, 1915
4   *Coventry Herald*, 12th/13th March, 1915
5   *Midland Counties Tribune*, 15th January, 1915
6   *Nuneaton Observer*, 12th February, 1915
7   *Midland Daily Telegraph*, 8th February, 1915
8   *Banbury Advertiser*, 4th March, 1915

[9] *Nuneaton Observer*, 12th February, 1915

[10] *Coventry Graphic*, 5th February, 1915

[11] *Stratford Herald*, 29th January, 1915

[12] *Rugby Advertiser*, 16th January, 1915

[13] *Coventry Herald*, 26th/27th February, 1915

[14] *Nuneaton Observer*, 26th February, 1915

[15] *Coventry Graphic*, 5th March, 1915

[16] *Rugby Advertiser*, 30th January, 1915

[17] *Nuneaton Observer*, 14th May, 1915

[18] *Rugby Advertiser*, 27th February, 1915

[19] Rev. Oswin Creighton: "With the 29th Division at Gallipoli", Longmans, Green and Co., 1916

[20] *Stratford Herald*, 22nd January, 1915

[21] *Stratford Herald*, 19th February, 1915

[22] Rev. Oswin Creighton: op. cit.

[23] *Rugby Advertiser*, 22nd May, 1915

[24] I am indebted to David Llewellyn for the information on Serjeant Johnston.

[25] *Nuneaton Observer*, 15th January, 1915

9

The Soldiers and Local Girls

CB

Wives …

With chances of re-acquaintance with family life curtailed, it is not surprising that men sought and often found some compensation in the domestic arrangements afforded by billeting. Inevitably, relationships were struck up between soldiers and local girls. Some even resulted in marriage.

On 16th January, the *Rugby Advertiser* reported one member of the Royal Inniskilling Fusiliers who had already "met his fate" and was intending "to lead a local lady to the altar at an early date". The edition for 13th March records the marriage, at the Registry Office, of Lance-Corporal Henry Tinmouth, of the Border Regiment, and Caroline Flavell, of 61 Railway Terrace, in Rugby. Aubrey Williams, Adjutant to the South Wales Borderers, noted that "a number of Coventry girls found their husbands from members of the Regiment"[1] The *Coventry Herald* for 12th/13th March said that it was understood that nine Borderers and two Munster Fusiliers had married during their stay in Coventry, although these figures did not include those married by the Church of England. During one week, a local firm had supplied carriages for eight weddings involving soldiers. At Nuneaton, Oswin Creighton was informed in February of some 30 soldiers being married in the registry office but found, on inquiry, that only nine licences had been issued. "Things do get so exaggerated", he observed.[2] As the time approached for the troops to leave there were further stories of Dublins marrying local girls.

Others used their time in the area to marry a girl from another part of the country to whom they had become engaged. On 23rd January, Corporal Ellis, of the Royal Field Artillery, married Miss Emily Robinson, at Leamington Parish Church. The bride came from Chelmsford. The bride and groom were drawn to the church by a gun team and members of the bridegroom's battery formed an archway of swords.[3] On 10th March, Sergeant John Bower, 1st West Riding Field Company, Royal Engineers, married Miss Wingfield from Sheffield, at the Parish Church in Long Itchington. Bower also came from Sheffield. A special licence had been obtained for the marriage. Sergeant Bower's unit left the area on 17th March and Mrs Bower would never see her husband again.

Whilst information on marriages involving ordinary soldiers and local girls is difficult to find, marriages involving officers usually got more publicity. On 5th March, Captain Arthur Pepys, 1st Battalion Essex Regiment, married Miss Olive Starkey at Banbury. Miss Starkey came from Bodicote House, in Banbury, and local Red Cross nurses and Boy Scouts provided the guard of honour. On 11th March, 2nd Lieutenant Timothy Sullivan, 1st Battalion Royal Munster Fusiliers, married Miss Maud Bates, at St Osburg's Church in Coventry. Miss Bates came from Albany Road, in the Earlsdon area of Coventry. Sullivan's best man was

38. *2nd Lieutenant Timothy Sullivan and Maud Bates, on their wedding day; Coventry, 11th March, 1915. Sullivan's best man was 2nd Lieutenant J. Watts.* (© Coventry Graphic)

2nd Lieutenant J. Watts; both had been promoted from the rank of Company Sergeant Major in February. Officers also took the opportunity to marry fiancées from another part of the country. Thus, Lieutenant T.H.O. Crawley, of the 4th Battalion Worcestershire Regiment, married Miss Meta Grant at Banbury on 6th February; Miss Grant had travelled from Perthshire for the wedding. Leave-takings for these and other couples came quickly and must have been painful. "What a mercy it is to be a bachelor on these occasions" was Oswin Creighton's view.[4]

… and sweethearts

In other cases, an arrangement would be made that would be furthered when the soldier returned after the war – "to claim the sweethearts left behind".[5] Some examples are given in Section 15, although many of these 'understandings' ended prematurely with the death of the soldier during the war.

Other relationships were, no doubt, of a more casual nature, although invariably a source of mutual pleasure. Predictably, there were those, especially among the clergy, who were worried at the potential for 'misconduct'. Such concerns seem usually to have been part of a more general unease at the effect of the war on the country's moral standards. The Bishop of Worcester, an avowed opponent of "free love", railed against "the dangerous system of billeting", by which girls were likely to become mothers. A firm believer in "a society of pure women", he was certain that some of the talk girls heard from billeted soldiers "was an imputation on the large majority of clean-minded men who made up the British Army".[6] The Bishop's views applied to the billeting process in general, rather than specifically to that of the 29th Division. He appears not to have produced any practical suggestions as to alternative arrangements for accommodating the large numbers of soldiers then present in the country. The Vicar of St Paul's, Warwick,

39. *Stockingford Church: where Oswin Creighton urged the Royal Fusiliers to do all they could to help the local girls.* (© Warwickshire County Record Office)

the Rev. E.H. Longland, shared at least some of the Bishop's concerns, speaking out in his parish magazine about the "giddy, unmaidenly girls in the streets", and expressing his amazement as to the "depths of immodesty they can fall". However, this was part of a general condemnation of contemporary behaviour, including thriftlessness and drink.[7] The Vicar of Kenilworth, the Rev. James Cairns, was somewhat more relaxed in his views but still expressed regret at the behaviour "of a few of our less steady young people. It is not a pleasant sight to see young women deliberately trying to attract the attention of the soldiers", although he was pleased that, in many cases, "they were promptly snubbed by the men themselves".[8]*

Somewhat closer to the soldiers themselves was Chaplain 4th Class, Oswin Creighton, whose views on a variety of matters have already been quoted. The son of the late Mandell Creighton, Bishop of London from 1897 to 1901, Oswin was appointed Anglican Chaplain to the 86th Brigade and arrived at the Divisional Headquarters, in Leamington, on 27th January, before moving to Nuneaton. He was not a member of the regular army and had previously been acting as a chaplain in a New Army brigade, where he had felt at home, mixing with officers who had come from a similar school and college background and who were equally unfamiliar with army life. He was daunted by the prospect of dealing with the "smart and seasoned" regulars, with their long-established traditions. His anxiety can only have been increased when a "talkative corporal" soon informed him that the men were not at all religious. Nonetheless, Oswin took his new responsibilities seriously and was particularly concerned with the moral welfare of his charges: "The men seem to be well-behaved, but of course in a town of this size there must be much that is wrong", he wrote on 29th January. On the following Sunday (31st January), he was determined to use his first church parade, at Stockingford Church with the Royal Fusiliers, to warn the men not to take advantage of the local women and girls, who had never had the military stationed in the area before and "were naturally very excited". Oswin Creighton must have

---

*   However, lest it be thought that the clergy were more concerned with the safeguarding of moral standards than they were with the well-being of soldiers soon to depart for active service, it should be pointed out that some of the most generous tributes to the men of the 29th Division came from the local clergy.

been somewhat put out when a good many of the soldiers arrived in the church with the women and girls in question. He insisted that the ladies should leave, so that he could address the soldiers 'man-to-man', urging them to do all they could to help the girls, "so that the memory they left behind them should always be of the good they have done during their stay". However, he does not seem to have regarded the occasion as a success, observing: "I am afraid the men do not like Church Parade."

Undaunted, on 2nd February, Oswin Creighton decided to investigate stories of soldiers leaving their billets at late hours to meet up with local girls. His investigations included an hour's walk along the canal towpath, beginning at 10.30 p.m.; fortunately, "it was a lovely moonlight night". However, apart from encountering a few soldiers "behaving quite orderly in the streets", in one or two cases with girls, he found nothing untoward. He also discovered that the men were actually allowed out until midnight. He also received assurance from "one of the other vicars", who had been out for three nights and had also seen nothing. Clearly relieved, Oswin felt that he could contradict a lot of the reports that were going about: "The men seem to be behaving very well."[9] A rather different view was put forward by Lieutenant Douglas Talbot, 1st Battalion Lancashire Fusiliers, who observed: "Our men are having the time of their lives in their billets; the whole place swarms with very pretty hat factory girls." He thought that "in 9 months time there should be the makings of a new army in Nuneaton alone".[10]

However, the longer term impact of liaisons between soldiers and local girls may not have been quite as dramatic as Lieutenant Douglas predicted. In October 1915, Dr Wood, the Deputy Medical Officer for Nuneaton, presented his monthly report to Nuneaton Council, which showed the local birth rate for September as 25 per 1,000, a continuation of its steady decline. The Mayor's jocular comment, that "We have not had the war babies yet", was met with laughter.[11] However, the rate showed only a slight increase to 26 and 27 per 1,000 in the reports for November and December and stood at just over 26 in the report submitted in January. At the meeting in November, Mrs Davies, the Health Visitor, reported that up until 30th November there had been 23 illegitimate babies in her district during 1915, by comparison with 24 during 1914.[12] The statistics for Coventry are similar, with the birth rate for 1915 at 23.8, down from 27.3 for 1914 and a continuation of a longer term decline. The number of registered illegitimate births stood at 1.9% of the total, by comparison with 2% in 1914. Clearly, the absence of many local men in the armed forces affected the birth rate but it would also appear that the presence of the 29th Division in Nuneaton and Coventry may not have given the local rates quite the stimulus that some had anticipated. As Oswin Creighton had observed about the number of marriages, "Things do get so exaggerated".

"Things like that"

More disturbing is the suggestion by Private Robert Bird, 147th Brigade, Royal Field Artillery, that "nearly all the men from India had gonorrhoea and things like that". Bird was a wartime volunteer and may have exaggerated rumours about the regulars; he certainly "always steered clear of them".[13] Nonetheless, his unit periodically had "short arm inspections" and the incidence of venereal disease was a recognised problem amongst regular soldiers, as it was amongst the civilian population at that time.[†]

[†] Nonetheless, the Report of the Royal Commission on Venereal Disease, 1916, concluded that the rate for venereal diseases in the army had fallen from 224.5 per 1,000 in 1888 to 56.5 per 1,000 in 1912, with the proportion of gonorrhoea to syphilis being 3:2. This decline was reflected in other European armies. The Commission's conclusions on the incidence of venereal diseases in the civilian population were more tentative. However, Wassermann tests on just over 1,000 patients at the London Hospital, undergoing treatment for reasons wholly unconnected with syphilis, showed 10.3% of the males and 5.1% of the females gave positive reactions.

However, the effect that the presence of the troops may have had on the local population in this respect appears to be difficult, if not impossible, to establish. Local statistics for the treatment for venereal diseases only began to appear in 1917, following the regulations issued by the Local Government Board in July 1916, which made it compulsory for councils of counties and county boroughs to make provision for the prevention and treatment of the diseases. Clearly, the introduction of such regulations indicates growing concern on the part of the Government, reflecting the conclusions of the 1916 Report of the Royal Commission on Venereal Disease, but this was general to the country as a whole, rather than specific to certain localities. In the case of Coventry, the number of cases being treated for such diseases more than trebled from 1917 to 1918, with the large majority being men.[14] However, it is not easy to draw conclusions from such figures, given the very large numbers of workers, both male and female, who moved to the city during the war, from many different parts of the country, to find employment in the munitions industries. Moreover, the increased numbers of people seeking treatment may, in part, be explained by the growing awareness that such treatment was available.

Just as it is difficult to establish how many marriages actually took place, other aspects of the relationships involving soldiers and local girls are also difficult to quantify. However, there seems no doubt as to the regrets felt by the soldiers when they moved away for "the dear girls we have left behind us".[15] No doubt such sentiments were frequently reciprocated.

&

[1]   Major General A.E. Williams CBE, DSO, MC; IWM DOCS 88/56/1; quoted in Nigel Steel and Peter Hart, "Defeat at Gallipoli"; Macmillan London, 1994
[2]   Rev. Oswin Creighton: "With the 29th Division at Gallipoli"; Longmans, Green and Co., 1916
[3]   *Warwick Advertiser*, 30th January, 1915
[4]   Oswin Creighton: op cit
[5]   From a poem by a soldier of the 1st Battalion Essex Regiment, printed in the *Banbury Advertiser*, 1st July, 1915
[6]   *Warwick Advertiser*, 9th May, 1915. The Bishop's comments were made at the opening of the Girls' Friendly Society Lodge at Coventry.
[7]   *Warwick Advertiser*, 13th March, 1915
[8]   *Coventry Herald*, 2nd/3rd April, 1915, quoting from the April issue of the St Nicholas Parish Magazine
[9]   Rev. Oswin Creighton: op cit
[10]   Capt A.D. Talbot, ms letters, letter to Captain T. Slingsby, 3 February, 1915; IWM DOCS, quoted in Nigel Steel and Peter Hart: op cit
[11]   *Nuneaton Observer*, 15th October, 1915
[12]   *Nuneaton Observer*, 10th December, 1915
[13]   Robert Bird; IWM SR 10656, quoted in Nigel Steel and Peter Hart: op cit
[14]   City of Coventry: Annual Reports of the Medical Officer of Health, 1915-18; Coventry History Centre, JN 352.4
[15]   Letter in *Rugby Advertiser*, 10th April, 1915

10

Problems

CB

Drink

After the departure from the area of the 29th Division, a poem entitled "The Floating Division" appeared in some of the local newspapers. Composed by "A Fusilier", the poem recounts how the Division had "floated gently" back to England, where:

> "By the English "civvies" we were scarcely understood,
> With jargon from the jungle and kultur from the Khud.
> But "thumbs up" was the signal, as we knew of course it would.
> And at every pub we halted, why the liquor was in flood.
> We floated to the pictures and we floated on parade,
> We floated in our billets, and friends were quickly made,
> And for nine long weeks each evening, in our beds we gently laid,
> The 29th Division and the 86th Brigade."

Subsequently, the Division would "float" back East and, after eight months of steering clear of the war, had finally "to put the pace on for the months we were delayed".[1]

Given the traditional fondness of many soldiers for alcohol, it was the most widely anticipated problem and local residents were warned against treating soldiers; this was in accordance with the Defence of the Realm Act (D.O.R.A.). The Act was also invoked to restrict the opening hours of public houses and registered clubs. These would now usually shut at 10 p.m. on weekdays, although in Banbury they were closed to soldiers from 9 p.m., perhaps reflecting the influence of local temperance workers, who had met in advance of the troops' arrival in order to lobby the authorities.[2] These measures may have reduced the scale of the problem but they never totally eliminated it.

For many soldiers the temptations were particularly strong following their arrival in the billeting area after a long sea voyage. In Banbury, a correspondent in the *Banbury Guardian* alleged that, after the arrival of the Worcestershire Regiment, "many scenes of drunkenness were witnessed".[3] (However, the letter writer, Geo. R. Forde, was involved in a dispute with the local licensing authorities, whom he felt were unduly lenient, and may have exaggerated his claims.) According to Lieutenant Guy Nightingale, 1st Battalion Royal Munster Fusiliers, "the men were frightfully drunk the first night". One Fusilier who got into trouble was Michael Walsh, who appeared in court on Tuesday morning, 12th January, charged with being drunk and disorderly in Little Park Street. At the suggestion of the Chief Constable, he was handed over to the military authorities. He was not alone: another six Munsters appeared in court on the same day, mainly charged with being drunk and incapable. They too were handed over to the military authorities, an arrangement that a military representative said was satisfactory to the Army. However, the Chairman of the Court thought that licensed victuallers should be warned to be careful when serving the soldiers.

In February, the licensee of the Binswood Tavern, in Leamington, was charged with selling intoxicating liquor to a soldier who was already drunk. The case came to rest upon whether the soldier was drunk "from a military point of view" and was eventually dismissed. Its significance, perhaps, is that the charges had been brought at the insistence of the Division's Provost and the incident came to light when a detail of men from the RHA had been instructed to search local pubs for men who were absent from duty. When the time came for the Division to leave the area, temporary restrictions were introduced to keep soldiers away from licensed premises in the remaining hours of their stay.

Drink could, of course, fuel violence, though recorded examples of violent conduct among billeted soldiers are comparatively few. In Warwick, in January, there was "a serious disturbance between civilians and soldiers". The details, however, were not reported and the incident may not have involved men from the 29th Division. In Nuneaton, a young local man, Arthur Daulman, would later recall the animosity between the Royal Dublin Fusiliers and "another regiment in the town", which produced at least one fracas in a local hostelry, the encounter at the Red Lion only being broken up with difficulty.[4] This was presumably the "Free Fight in Queen's Road on Saturday Night" referred to in the *Midland Counties Tribune* for 26th February. If so, it involved "scores" of soldiers from all three battalions billeted in Nuneaton and Stockingford! The trouble started in the yard outside a public house just after 9 p.m. and resulted in "a very lively five minutes". The military and civilian police had to be called in to restore order. A parson also appeared on the scene and a doctor was summoned to deal with one of the "combatants" who had "come in for a little rough usage". The military police made several arrests. Unfounded rumours later circulated that one of the soldiers had died.

Other incidents were on a smaller scale. On 26th January, Private John Moore, Royal Dublin Fusiliers, was charged with being drunk and disorderly in Coton Road. Police Constable Phillips said Moore was fighting with a civilian. Moore's defence was that he had had no beer for 18 months and a quantity had overcome him. He was discharged on promise that he would leave the drink alone.[5] On 6th March, a Lancashire Fusilier, Private Herbert Godfrey, appeared before Coventry magistrates, charged with being drunk and disorderly at Bedworth the previous day and with assaulting a policeman. On his arrest, Godfrey stated that he was a Lancashire Lad and that no policeman in Bedworth could lock him up; whereupon he kicked P.C. Malin. Although the magistrates were willing to let the military authorities deal with the matter, no reply was received from them and Malin re-appeared before the court on the 9th, being fined 10s, plus costs, the total amounting to £1 6d. Nor did the military authorities intervene to help Private Patrick O'Connor, 1st Battalion Royal Munster Fusiliers, who was convicted of an assault on P.C. James Pearce, at Coventry on 6th March. Indeed, a character reference obtained from the commanding officer showed that the prisoner, who had served for more than five years in the Army, had a poor record and was "a bad lot". He was sentenced to three months hard labour, a conviction that would mean, of course, that he missed his Battalion's departure for the Dardanelles.[6]

Soon after the arrival of the troops in Nuneaton, it was claimed that "in one of the battalions ... nearly 75% are total abstainers"[7]. Although this appears to have been rather optimistic, the Division did contain soldiers who belonged to the temperance movement. The two infantry battalions billeted in Coventry had lodges in the International Order of Good Templars – 'The Munsters' Pride' and 'The Rorke's Drift' – and these were active during their stay in the city. There were also lodges reported in Leamington, Rugby and Nuneaton. In Rugby, Sergeant Mudd, of the 1st Battalion Royal Inniskilling Fusiliers, whose contribution to the Home Mission is mentioned in Section 8, was keen to refute a statement that had appeared in the local newspaper that half of the members of the Military Good Templar Lodge had broken their pledge on the homeward voyage. Of the Lodge's 66 members in India, he claimed that 57 were still on the books.[8]

As noted, the military authorities took steps to police their own men and thus dealt with many incidents without the involvement of the civil authorities. Moreover, the local courts seem to have been keen to hand soldiers back to the Army for punishment. But, even taking these factors into account, there were remarkably few recorded cases of violence, or even of drunkenness, especially when one considers the number of troops stationed in the area. Coventry's Chief Constable reported that, despite the large number of soldiers in the city, their conduct had not increased the rate of drunkenness and generally there had been little disorder.[9] His opinion was echoed by the Chief Constable of Leamington who said that it was impossible to speak too highly of the behaviour of the troops stationed in the town.[10] It was also noted with satisfaction that pickets were not needed to monitor the nocturnal behaviour of the soldiers in Kenilworth[11] and, when the 2nd Hampshires left Stratford, it was stated that not a single case of misconduct had needed the attention of the police during their stay.[12]

However, the legend of 'The Floating Division' was far from being a complete fabrication. It was rumoured, for example, that the premature departure from Nuneaton of the Royal Dublin Fusiliers and the Royal Fusiliers on 6th March (see Section 11) was a consequence of the considerable opportunities in the town for obtaining drink. The *Nuneaton Observer* commented that this was "a matter known only to the authorities", adding that "it is stated that the punishment list of the Dublins during their stay in Nuneaton was unprecedented".[13]

A glimpse into the drinking habits of billeted soldiers was offered by the inquest into Benjamin Bird, a miner from Stockingford. Bird, who had been "drinking very heavily for three weeks", was found dead from exposure on the morning of Saturday, 23rd January, in the garden of his house in Herbert Street. The previous day, he had come home in the late afternoon, "under the influence of drink", before going out again. During the evening his drinking companions included two members of the Royal Fusiliers, Privates Walter Porter and William Brightwell. Having left the White Lion at about 9 pm, Porter accompanied Bird to a house in Croft Road, where Bird had a drink of whisky, although not Porter. They left the house at 10.30, with Bird declining Porter's offer to see him home. They parted company but Bird only got as far as the outside of his washhouse. At the inquest, Brightwell expressed the opinion that Bird had certainly had enough to drink but he thought him capable of getting home safely.[14] The picture that emerges is of soldiers who mixed freely with civilians in the local pubs but who were usually capable of holding their liquor and knowing their limits.

Other Problems

There were, of course, other problems. On 19th February, a case came before Banbury Borough Police Court in which a local man was fined for receiving three pairs of army boots from Private B. Rogers, 1st Battalion Essex Regiment, in the knowledge that they had been stolen. Rogers had taken the boots, which were brand new, from three of his comrades, who duly appeared in court to identify their property. Rogers was dealt with by the military authorities: he was court-martialled and sentenced to 84 days imprisonment. The local man was fined.[15] On 9th March, Privates Daniel McGregor and Hugh MacCheyne, of the King's Own Scottish Borderers, appeared before the Rugby Petty Sessions charged with the theft of a ham from the Crown Inn at Newbold. Their defence – that they were drunk and had been given the ham – was not believed. A captain from the Regiment said that the character of both men was bad. MacCheyne was sent to prison for a month, McGregor for two weeks – both with hard labour. A week later, Privates Albert Ince and James Boxhall, of the South Wales Borderers, also appeared before the Rugby Petty Sessions charged with theft, in this case of 12 pairs of men's trousers, stolen from outside a shop in Chapel Street, Rugby. The men subsequently tried to sell the trousers at the Royal Oak in Dunchurch Road. Again, the prisoners claimed they were drunk and had been given the stolen goods by someone else. They too were not believed and, once again, the regiment concerned did not support the men – indeed the Colonel telephoned the Police to say that there was nothing in favour of either of them and there were previous convictions against them. Ince was dealt with lightly – bound over for the sum of £1 – but Boxhall was given three months hard labour, reduced to two on account of the fact that he had been at the front and had been wounded. The theft of the trousers had taken place on the evening of 12th March, a few hours after the King's inspection of the 29th Division.

Even officers occasionally transgressed, such as Lieutenant Lawrence Boustead of the Royal Dublin Fusiliers, who was fined 10s for riding a motor cycle in Nuneaton without a light. The defendant did not appear in court, however, but sent a letter to the bench.[16] Another problem is suggested by the notices that Lieutenant-Colonel F.G. Jones, Royal Inniskilling Fusiliers, placed in the *Rugby Advertiser* for three consecutive weeks, advising the people of Rugby that the pay of soldiers could not be stopped for the recovery of private debts and that "if the inhabitants allow soldiers to contract debts, they will do so at their own risk".

There were also issues relating to the standard of billeting, although the scale of these problems is not entirely clear. The *Nuneaton Observer* hinted that there were some households in which soldiers were not adequately fed, as unscrupulous hosts pocketed more than their fair share of the billeting allowance, although the paper also recognised that in many cases soldiers received more than their entitlement. In Stratford, a somewhat

40. *Landladies queuing to claim unpaid billeting allowances; Little Park Street, Coventry, 29th March, 1915.* (© Coventry Graphic)

tetchy correspondence followed the publication of a letter in which a resident of Shottery claimed that some hostesses were serving the soldiers with cold meals and tinned food, in order to save themselves the trouble of cooking wholesome hot dishes. These claims provoked criticism and "contented" soldiers wrote to testify as to the adequacy of their billets. The *Stratford Herald* did, however, acknowledge that there had been a few cases in which soldiers had not been provided with proper food; as already noted, the "miserly people" responsible had been punished by the soldiers being re-billeted. A related matter was the failure of the military authorities in Coventry to pay all billeting allowances punctually. Several hundred landladies in the Earlsdon area were affected and complaints were made to the police. A photograph in the *Coventry Graphic* shows a sizeable queue of landladies in Little Park Street, waiting to claim what they were owed.[17]

Health

The winter weather was trying for men recently removed from hot climates. Oswin Creighton recorded that most of the Lancashire Fusiliers had been in India a long time and felt the cold but were getting acclimatised.[18] Several men from the Royal Field Artillery were soon admitted to the Warneford Hospital in Leamington.[19] The Warneford was a peacetime hospital now called upon to deal with military patients and the presence of the military in the area would result in "a large influx of cases" at the Hospital.[20] Some soldiers were suffering from malaria and doctors at Nuneaton were soon examining the men, with a few being sent to hospital at Tuttle Hill. The *Stratford Herald* reported that "sickness very largely prevailed" among the Hampshires in the early part of their stay but "as the weeks rolled on a gradual improvement manifested itself" and that, when the time came for men to leave the town, "very few remained on the sick list".[21] Subsequently, the Division's Principal Medical Officer was generous in his praise of the local VAD units, with the Town Hall Hospital in Stratford being described as "a model of its kind".[22] Similar expressions of gratitude would be made to the other hospitals in the area. It would appear that an allowance of 3s a day was paid by the War Office for each soldier in hospital.[23]

Overall, the health of the Division's soldiers appears to have improved significantly during their stay. Looking back, Lance-Corporal Clarke, 4th Battalion Worcestershire Regiment, commented: "There was a vast difference noticeable in the build of each man on the day they left Banbury than on the day of arrival. If it was from pleasant homes or Banbury cakes, I cannot say."[24]

Inevitably, some men were injured in training. The Clarendon VAD Hospital at Kineton had to deal with a number of minor injuries suffered by the 2nd West Riding Field Company of the Royal Engineers. These included one man who was kicked by a horse, and Charles Dunstan, who was accidentally shot by a revolver fired by one of his comrades; he was immediately conveyed to the Hospital, where he was described as "progressing favourably".[25] A gunshot wound was also sustained by Private Dyball, 1st Battalion Royal Dublin Fusiliers, who shot himself in the knee on the morning of the Dublins' move from Nuneaton to Kenilworth. Dyball was handling his gun in an outhouse in Edward Street when it went off. The soldier had an excellent record – well-behaved and abstemious – and it was assumed that the incident was a genuine accident, although "the point which remains mysterious is why the gun was loaded at the time". He was taken to Nuneaton General Hospital; although his injuries were not too serious, they would have prevented him from sailing with the Division.[26]

A health problem that may not have been anticipated was an outbreak of equine influenza in Nuneaton, the source of which was attributed to the Army horses. "Many military horses were accommodated in the Stockingford area and influenza made its appearance in every stable in that locality, a number of cases proving fatal." Eight horses belonging to Nuneaton Council were affected, two of them being in a "sad condition".[27]

Fatalities

There were five fatalities among the soldiers during their stay in the area. The first was Private Sidney Earley, 2nd Battalion Hampshire Regiment, who died of pneumonia in the Town Hall Hospital in Stratford-upon-Avon on 5th February. Two weeks before his death, he had captained the Battalion football XI in their game against Stratford. He was 27 years old, "a genial, virile and popular comrade", according to the *Stratford Herald*. Six members of the team acted as pall bearers at his funeral and the route from the Parish Church to the cemetery was lined with hundreds of civilians. The Battalion's drum and fife band played "Flowers of the Forest", as his comrades slow-marched to the cemetery. Earley came from Winchester and his father, sister and brothers were present at the funeral. Three volleys were fired over his grave and the Last Post was played. "Many years have rolled by since a military funeral of similar proportions was witnessed in the borough", stated the *Herald*.[28] Private Earley had been in hospital for more than a week and was one of many soldiers in the town who were suffering from illness at that time, with a dozen or so being treated in hospital. In April, a memorial stone was erected in the cemetery. This was partly paid for by Earley's comrades and the design included the regimental crest.

Another pneumonia victim was Private James McGhee, 1st Battalion Royal Dublin Fusiliers, who died at Tuttle Hill Hospital, in Nuneaton, on 9th February.[*] He was 30 years old and had been in Nuneaton little more than a week, having arrived as part of a draft of 79 from the Regimental barracks at Cork. His mother travelled from Glasgow for the funeral and he was buried with full military honours at St Joseph's Roman Catholic Church. McGhee belonged to 'D' Company and the full complement of officers and men turned out to honour his memory. An advance party accompanied the coffin as it was brought from the hospital, the soldiers marching with rifles reversed. At one point, they encountered platoons of the Lancashire Fusiliers, with their band playing a lively march. The officer in command of the Lancashires immediately silenced the band, gave the command "Eyes Right" and saluted the coffin in the name of the platoons. Large crowds of civilians watched the cortège pass. At Princes Street corner, the remainder of 'D' Company fell in. The "Dead March" was played during the final stage of the journey. The public were prevented from entering the church and the grounds, although children from the Catholic school lined one side of the pathway to the church, with Fusiliers on the other. Following the service and burial, three volleys from 12 rifles were fired over the grave and buglers sounded the Last Post. The coffin contained the inscription "James McGhee, died February 9th, 1915, No. 17071 R.I.P."[29] The *Nuneaton Observer* considered that "this is the only record which we believe exists for a purely military funeral within the borough".[30]

Lieutenant Arthur Devas, 1st Battalion Essex Regiment, died at St Peter-in-the-East, part of the 3rd General Military Hospital, in Oxford, on 15th February. He had returned to his billet in Banbury after a few days leave but complained of feeling unwell and was immediately sent to Oxford, where he lapsed into unconsciousness. After lying in a coma for three days, he died on the evening of 15th February.[†] The cause of death was diabetes. He was 37 years old, had served in the Boer War and had been commissioned from the ranks. His body was returned home and he was buried at Minehead Cemetery, in Somerset.

---

[*]   The Commonwealth War Graves Commission gives the date of death as 10th February.

[†]   The Commonwealth War Graves Commission gives the date of death as 1st February; however, the death certificate for Arthur Devas shows 15th February, which accords with the information in the *Banbury Guardian* for 18th February and with the 'Officers Died' database.

41. *The graves of Privates James Macdonald (King's Own Scottish Borderers) and Stewart Gardner (Royal Inniskilling Fusiliers), Clifton Road Cemetery, Rugby.* (© Author)

Two men billeted in Rugby died there. On 8th March, Private James Macdonald of the King's Own Scottish Borderers died at Ashlawn Red Cross Hospital in the town. He had been admitted 24 hours previously and had been assessed by medical officers of the 87th Field Ambulance. The peculiar smell of the man's breath suggested diabetes, and this was confirmed by examination of a urine sample.[31] Unfortunately, the coma into which Private Macdonald had slipped deepened and he died the following morning. (The cause of death was confirmed as diabetes.) James Macdonald was 23 years old and came from Glasgow. His mother travelled to Warwickshire for the funeral, as did one of his brothers who was recovering from wounds received whilst serving with the BEF. Another three brothers were in the army. Private Macdonald was also buried with full military honours and large numbers of local people, as well as many soldiers, lined the route taken by the cortège to the cemetery in Clifton Road. A firing party fired three volleys at the graveside and pipers and drummers from his Regiment played 'Loch Habberd no more'. The ceremony was "one of the most unique of its kind ever seen in Rugby".[32]

Equally unfortunate was 26 years old Private Stewart Gardner of the Royal Inniskilling Fusiliers, who died on 31st March, after the Division had left for overseas service. He had just returned to his lodgings from a spell in hospital with pneumonia. He was looking forward to a month's furlough and had arranged a rail pass at the local station. After dinner, he sat talking with his landlady before asking if he might go to his bedroom to collect his belongings. Unfortunately, having done so, he fell down the stairs and fractured his skull. He never regained consciousness and died the same evening in hospital. The conclusion of the inquest was that Gardner was sober at the time of the accident but the stairs were described as "steep and dark", with an initial "drop step", about which he may simply have forgotten during his time away from the house. Although a number of his family came from Belfast, there was to be no military funeral for Private Gardner – his Battalion had arrived at Alexandria, in Egypt, by the time he was buried in Clifton Road Cemetery.[33]

CB

1   *Leamington Courier*, 15th October, 1915

2   *Banbury Guardian*, 6th May, 1915

3   *Banbury Guardian*, 6th May, 1915.

4   James Sambrook, "With the Rank and Pay of a Sapper"; Paddy Griffith Associates, 1998

5   *Nuneaton Observer*, 29th January, 1915

6   *Coventry Herald*, 9th/10th April, 1915

7   *Nuneaton Observer*, 15th January, 1915

8   *Rugby Advertiser*, 23rd January, 1915

9   *Coventry Herald*, 12th February, 1915

10   *Leamington Courier*, 12th March, 1915

11   *Coventry Herald*, 5th February, 1915

12   *Stratford Herald*, 12th March, 1915

13   *Nuneaton Observer*, 12th March, 1915

14   *Nuneaton Observer*, 29th January, 1915

15   *Banbury Guardian*, 25th February, 1915

16   *Nuneaton Observer*, 26th February, 1915

17   *Coventry Graphic*, 2nd April, 1915

18   Oswin Creighton, "With 29th Division in Gallipoli"; Longmans, Green and Co., 1916

19   *Leamington Courier*, 1st January, 1915

20   *Leamington Courier*, 16th April, 1915

21   *Stratford Herald*, 12th March, 1915.

22   *Stratford Herald*, 7th May, 1915

23   *Stratford Herald*, 15th October, 1915

24   *Banbury Advertiser*, 10th June, 1915

25   *Warwick Advertiser*, 20th February, 1915

26   *Nuneaton Observer*, 12th March, 1915

27   *Nuneaton Observer*, 30th April, 1915 and *Warwick Advertiser*, 1st May, 1915

28   *Stratford Herald*, 12th February, 1915

29   *Midland Counties Tribune*, 12th February, 1915

30   *Nuneaton Observer*, 12th February, 1915

31   War Diary of the 87th Field Ambulance Brigade; National Archives WO 95/4309

32   *Rugby Advertiser*, 13th March, 1915

33   *Rugby Advertiser*, 10th April, 1915

11

The Final Two Weeks

☙

The concentration of the Division

In early March, there was some movement of units within the billeting area, aimed at a more central concentration of the Division's forces. Its primary purpose was "in accordance with a Divisional Scheme for bringing the formations in more convenient groups for training purposes".[1] It was also prior to the King's inspection of the Division on 12th March and the departure of the Division for service overseas (a process that began on 15th March).

Several battalions changed their billets on 5th and 6th March, with the 1st Essex and 4th Worcesters leaving Banbury for Warwick and Leamington, the 2nd Hampshires leaving Stratford for Warwick, the 1st Royal Dublin Fusiliers leaving Nuneaton for Kenilworth and the 2nd Royal Fusiliers moving from Stockingford to Coventry. To make room for the Royal Fusiliers in Coventry, the 2nd South Wales Borderers moved from the city to Rugby on 5th

42. *An indistinct shot of Royal Engineers in Kineton: the photograph was taken by the daughter of the village schoolmaster on a Brownie camera and the image was only recovered in the 1990s.*
(© Gillian Ashley-Smith)

March, thus completing the concentration of the 87th Brigade in that town. (The Borderers were billeted at New Bilton, on the outskirts of Rugby, some consolation for those there who felt they had been overlooked in the original billeting arrangements.) Finally, on the night of 10th/11th March, the 5th Royal Scots journeyed from Scotland to Leamington, thereby providing the Division's final infantry battalion.

Some of the smaller units moved as well. The 88th Field Ambulance left Coventry for Kenilworth, their place at Coventry being taken by the 89th Field Ambulance, who moved from Nuneaton. 'C' Squadron of the Surrey Yeomanry left Stratford for Barford. Two companies of the ASC left Kenilworth for Coventry. On 5th March, the 1st West Riding Field Company of the Royal Engineers left Kineton. About 240 men, accompanied by their baggage wagons, pontoons and other equipment, marched 10 or more miles to Long Itchington. It was "close upon 90 years" since soldiers had been billeted in the village and the arrangements that had become familiar in the other billeting centres were now repeated, as soldiers were shown to their quarters and equipment stored; the Schools were opened in the evening for use as recreation rooms, and so on. The troops soon made themselves at home and before long the hosts were praising their excellent behaviour and many good qualities.[2]

Understandably, the departure of so many units was an emotional time, as the soldiers said farewell to the communities in which they had been living for several weeks. There were "very animated scenes" as the men of the Essex and Worcestershire Regiments left Banbury on Friday, 5th March. Thousands turned out to watch them leave: first the Worcesters, at about 8.30 in the morning, and then the Essex Regiment, about half an hour later. As they marched from the town, the drums and bugles of both regiments played. The Worcesters formed "a compact body of men in their prime, swinging along with a firm, brisk tread, and shaping a sinuous course". Baggage was sent by rail but the marching troops were still followed by ammunition wagons, Maxim guns, horses and mules, ambulance vans, water tanks, and field kitchens, from which smoke emitted because they were in use. Nothing could have exceeded "the heartiness of the farewell" given to the Essex Regiment, with "handshakes and even more affectionate farewells". Some residents followed the troops for several miles, a few walking the whole distance to Warwick or Leamington. These included a number of children; they arrived too late to make the return journey and had to spend the night at Warwick Workhouse, their families being informed by telegram. The next day, soldiers could be seen having 'a whip round' to find the money to pay for the children's railway fares back to Banbury. Many Banbury people travelled to Warwick and Leamington on the following Sunday and some of the soldiers came back to Banbury on a short leave.[3]

With the departure of the troops, Banbury returned to normal but, in the opinion of the *Banbury Guardian*, "the sojourn of the 1st Essex and 4th Worcesters will live long in the memories of the present generation of Banburians. ... A closer acquaintance with the military caused a much higher opinion of the soldiers to be formed than has heretofore existed in the minds of those who knew 'Tommy Atkins' by repute." The newspaper also said of the departing troops what many no doubt thought: "One could not fail to speculate what the near future might have in store for many of the manly fellows then so full of life and high spirits."[4]

On the same day as the troops marched away from Banbury, the 2nd Battalion Hampshire Regiment left Stratford. Two days earlier, on Wednesday, 3rd March, they had been given 48 hours notice of their departure. On the Friday morning, a full dress parade of the Hampshires was held in the Rother Market and "all Stratford" turned out to watch, with hundreds lining Wood Street, Bridge Street and the Warwick Road. The military display "was one that had not before been witnessed in Stratford. The men were fully equipped, and from the accompanying impedimenta one obtained an idea of what is required in modern warfare." The soldiers "marched away with the debonair of brave men" and some of the local people "were frank enough to declare that they regretted the severance almost as deeply as if they had been their own flesh and blood". The severance was not final, however, as hundreds of the soldiers returned to Stratford on the Saturday and Sunday, making their way on foot, by bike or motor to spend a few hours in "agreeable company".[5] The Surrey Yeomanry had left the town on 4th March for Barford.

The scenes on Saturday, 6th March, that accompanied the departure from Nuneaton of the Royal Dublin Fusiliers and the Royal Fusiliers were, if anything, even more animated. "Never before in the history of Nuneaton has anything so extra-ordinary been witnessed."[6] The farewell to the Dublins was especially emotional – "these large-hearted, happy soldiers who have filled the town with good-humoured merriment" and who had "endeared themselves to the inhabitants". By the time they marched from the parade ground at 9.30 a.m., the streets were "thronged" and people immediately rushed forward to bid them 'good-bye'. Some of the soldiers were evidently the worse for drink and seemed "a trifle unsteady and out of step", although the more generous observers blamed their new boots. The Regimental band struck up a "lively air" and, from Coton Arches to Griff Hollows, "the Dubs marched through a thick avenue of several thousand people", who were drawn from all social classes. People clasped the hands of the soldiers and others bestowed kisses, with some of the soldiers proving, in this respect, "experts at '15 rounds rapid'". Not surprisingly, "the young womanhood of Nuneaton was predominant. ... It was the age of youth – the moment of youth." Although some "stern-faced matrons" looked on disapprovingly, others of the "married fraternity" viewed the scenes with a quiet acquiescence. Inevitably, 'Tipperary' was sung. In Edward Street, a large, powerful British bull-dog sat at one window, with a green ribbon round its neck; the soldiers cheered as they marched past, whilst "the dog looked on with a steady gaze". The soldiers swung along at pace – "a magnificent regiment on the march" – before disappearing over the hill beyond Griff Hollows. "How many of the laughing warriors will be left when victory has been achieved?" speculated the *Observer*.[7] Sadly, the answer would be "all too few".

43. *Members of the 2nd Battalion Hampshire Regiment at Stratford. Several men have long service stripes on their left sleeves.* (© Shakespeare Birthplace Trust)

44. *Sergeant Marsh of the Surrey Yeomanry in Stratford. Another yeoman and his horse appear from a passageway on the right, perhaps from the stables that were being used.* (© Shakespeare Birthplace Trust)

About 15 minutes later, the Royal Fusiliers joined the Griff Road, from the direction of Heath End and their billets in Stockingford. The 'Royals' were also received with acclamation: "a bright battalion and as they marched briskly along their faces were covered with smiles", with the soldiers eagerly shaking hands with civilians. By 11.30 a.m. the Dublins had arrived at Great Heath in Coventry, their march through the district again attracting large crowds of spectators. At Foleshill, they had received considerable quantities of cigarettes, and a little girl distributed several baskets of oranges. On the north side of Coventry, the Battalion made use of their field kitchens and stopped for refreshments before their journey, more akin to a triumphal march, was resumed. As they passed through Coventry, their band still played and 'Tipperary' was still sung, with some soldiers accompanying on their mouth organs. Again, large numbers watched as they passed down Bishop Street and through the centre of the city before continuing up Hertford Street on their way to Kenilworth. The Royal Fusiliers were also the recipients of cigarettes, fruit and sweets and entered into "good-natured chaffing with some of the onlookers". They were preceded by their band and drum and fife band as they made their way to the distributing centres in Coventry, from which the police showed them to their billets. An hour later, the 89th Field Ambulance, along with their equipment, arrived in the city from Nuneaton.[8]

As the Royal Dublin Fusiliers headed towards Kenilworth, two companies of the ASC who had been staying in that town were marching in the opposite direction to Foleshill, where the local police would direct them to their temporary billets. The arrival of more than a thousand Dublins in Kenilworth, along with their convoy drawn by about 100 horses, was again considered "a stirring sight", the Battalion occupying half a mile of roadway. Their 12 mile march from Nuneaton had been made with 60lb packs and rifles weighing some 9lbs. They were "the first and only regiment to have stayed in Kenilworth" but the initial arrangements did not find favour with them. "Kenilworth ... has very little attraction for the soldiers, who were keenly disappointed at leaving Nuneaton."[9] The notification of billeting requirements had been made at very short notice and it seems that the Kenilworth authorities had initially been told to expect two battalions and that this led to some unnecessary overcrowding in the billets that were used. Some of the Dublins were quick to make their displeasure known; on Saturday evening, and during the whole of Sunday, hundreds of them, joined by many of the Royal Fusiliers from Coventry, made their way back to their former billets in Nuneaton. Many walked, although the buses were crowded and brake proprietors "were not slow to see the opportunity for business". The inhabitants of Bedworth and other places along the route "stared in wonder at the spectacle" and "there was almost as much excitement at the return of the Fusiliers as there was at their departure".[10]

The *Nuneaton Observer* rounded on "the people of Kenilworth", who "cannot be congratulated upon the reception of the Dublins. The number of complaints is extraordinary." One soldier was "forced to sleep on boards, covered only by an overcoat; another was not allowed in the sitting rooms and had to retire to the sleeping apartment when in the house". Quite what soldiers then serving on the Western Front would have made of such hardships was not a subject for speculation by the paper, whose disparagement of Kenilworth continued apace: "These are splendid examples of a certain type of 'patriotism' which does a lot of shouting but gives no assistance to the nation's cause." Somewhat uncharitably, the *Observer* went on to suggest that: "A taste of German bombardment and pillaging might endow them with a gift of good manners." It would appear that more than a march of 12 miles separated the two towns. Not surprisingly, the townspeople of Kenilworth were taken aback by such attacks upon their hospitality and, in truth, the initial difficulties with respect to billeting were resolved and the Dublins would find their new accommodation more than satisfactory. The *Warwick Advertiser* was probably closer to the truth when it suggested Kenilworth lacked the places of amusement possessed by Nuneaton and that the larger town also had "a bigger population with which to 'chum up'".[11] No doubt it was a further opportunity to 'chum up' with Nuneaton's winsome young ladies that had proved a particular incentive to the peripatetic 'Dubs' and 'Royals'.

The arrival of the 4th Battalion Worcestershire Regiment at Leamington on 5th March was followed by that of the 5th Battalion Royal Scots, who travelled overnight from Edinburgh and arrived in Leamington on 11th March. The Royal Scots were billeted in the neighbourhood of the Campion Hills and appear to have enjoyed their brief stay. "We were billeted in private houses and treated like gentlemen."[12]

45. *The arrival in Leamington of the 5th Battalion Royal Scots; 11th March, 1915.* (© Alan Griffin)

The unannounced inspection

As the location of the monument to the 29th Division bears testimony, the inspection of the Division by King George V, on 12th March, 1915, is of unique importance in the history Warwickshire. It marks the spot at which one the most famous British divisions of the First World War came together for the first time and it reflects the intense interest taken by local people in these "soldier guests" and their subsequent experiences. Therefore it may seem strange to later generations that so few civilians witnessed the inspection and that so little was written about it in contemporary newspapers.

Undoubtedly, local people would have watched in considerable numbers, had they only known when and where the inspection was taking place. However, that knowledge was denied them by wartime censorship, in support of the King's wishes that he should be allowed to inspect his troops privately. These constraints also meant that very little was published after the event, beyond the reiteration of the Court Circular for 12th March, which simply stated that: "The King, attended by Major Clive Wigram, Vice-Admiral Sir Colin Keppel, and Lieutenant-Colonel Frank Dugdale, inspected troops in Southern Command to-day." Local newspapers were prevented, or believed they were prevented, from publishing more detailed accounts of the event. The *Coventry Graphic*, for example, made do with a photograph of civilians at the inspection point (which was not named), with the caption: "Where is it?" and the suggestion that "the spot should be of interest after the war".[13] The *Nuneaton Observer* complained that it had submitted "what we thought were very guarded reports to the Press Censor, but blank, blank, blank — all blank".[14] The paper's chagrin was made worse by the appearance of photographs of the event in Coventry.

The one newspaper that did break ranks was the normally staid *Leamington Courier*, which printed a report of the inspection on the day that it took place under a two column heading "The King And His Troops. (Special)". Whilst stopping short of actually naming the place of inspection, "this Friday morning all roads led to --", they dropped a fairly broad hint: "and if the Dun Cow was not there in spirit ..." This was an obvious allusion to Dunsmore Heath and the nearby Dun Cow Inn. However, to avoid any doubt, reference had already been made to the Brigade inspection near Stretton on Dunsmore and "the heath once ravaged by the Dun Cow". Even so, the *Courier's* coverage of the inspection

46. *The King in conversation with a battalion commanding officer, as he passes infantry (perhaps the 1st Battalion Lancashire Fusiliers) on 12th March, 1915. What appears to be a doffed hat from one of the civilian spectators can be seen on the right of the photo.* (© Albert Smith)

was only brief, largely restricted to the events that preceded the march-past, such as an accident to a military policeman, who was thrown from his horse; he was carried into a field where his broken leg was placed in splints by men from the RAMC, before being removed to hospital in the ambulance belonging to the Warwickshire Yeomanry. Most of the *Courier's* article was made up of background material on 'The King in Mufti', even though the King on the day appeared in military uniform. Perhaps the requirements of publication meant that the correspondent had to curtail his stay at the crossroads.

Not surprisingly, the *Courier's* effrontery annoyed other newspapers. The *Coventry Herald* stated that newspapers, both national and local, had mostly refrained from reporting the ceremony, beyond the official announcement, out of respect for the King's wishes, adding: "any journal which, for the sake of a trumpery journalistic 'scoop', has been reporting the inspection has done so in distinct breach of good faith with the authorities and its rivals". Somewhat sententiously, it also claimed some civilian spectators had butted their way in on the ceremony because "there will always be people vulgar and curious enough to 'mob' celebrities under any circumstances whatsoever".[15]

As has been seen, one of those "vulgar and curious" people was the Coventry-based journalist, Henry Wilkins, who regretted the censorship that denied so many local people the opportunity to witness or even to read about the inspection. "So it may be that the events of so much interest to Warwickshire folk who saw the inspection will only be recorded in private letters and in oral tradition handed down from sire to son."[16] Wilkins did not state how he heard in advance of the inspection but he did describe how, in the company of Annie and Martha Webb, he took the train to Brandon, on the morning of 12th March; the party then walked to the Dun Cow, on the London Road, near Stretton on Dunsmore. Although "all private and vehicular traffic was held up" in the direction of Dunchurch, he and his companions were able to reach the saluting point at the intersection of the London Road and the Fosse Way. He estimated that between 1,000 and 1,200 civilians eventually assembled there. Spectators were ordered into the fields on either side of the Fosse, to the south of its junction with the London Road, although others lined the gaps between the hedges and the roadway and a few even climbed up trees. More than 60 years later, Albert McConnell, a member of the Machine Gun Section

47. *George V inspecting the Division's artillery; London Road, 12th March, 1915.* (© Warwickshire County Record Office)

48. *Members of the 1ˢᵗ Battalion King's Own Scottish Borderers marching down the London Road towards the saluting point, 12ᵗʰ March, 1915. The photograph is part of a sequence apparently taken from the ditch on the south side of the road.* (© Warwickshire Library and Information Service)

of the 1ˢᵗ Battalion Royal Inniskilling Fusiliers, recalled a small incident that "caused a bit of a laugh" among his comrades. Whilst holding back the crowd, a young police officer placed his hands on the shoulders of some ladies. In response, one of them "started to brush her shoulder as if he had pipe clay on his white gloves".[17]

The King's inspection had been widely anticipated. Indeed, rumours to that effect were circulating in Rugby as early as January.[18] Preparations for the brigade inspections raised expectations. As the *Leamington Courier* reported, "On one occasion hundreds of pedestrians and cyclists hurried to Stoneleigh Deer Park, confident that his Majesty would appear before their expectant gaze" – this being the day of the inspection of the 87ᵗʰ Brigade near Stretton on Dunsmore. When the soldiers began to make themselves "as spick and span as possible" for 12ᵗʰ March, many local people concluded that the King must finally be coming.[19] Good numbers of civilians from Rugby, in particular, seem to have followed the departing troops. Finding the road blocked by the police at Dunchurch, many of them took to the fields to continue their progress.

49. *The King flanked by members of his entourage at the saluting point, 12ᵗʰ March, 1915. The party is positioned on "the triangular piece of greensward", which later became the site of the monument. The Fosse Way heading south lies behind the King. Does X mark the head of the person who took the photo on Page 16?* (© Paul Waller)

50. *The King and his Maudslay motor car; 12th March, 1915. The location cannot be identified; during the inspection, the King chose to remain on horseback.* (© Paul Waller)

Amongst the small number of local people who had at least some indication of coming events were those associated with Biggin Hall Farm at Thurlaston. Part of the Duke of Buccleuch's estate, the tenant farmer was John Mitchell, who had worked the land since 1903. In advance of the inspection, he was approached by the military authorities for temporary use of the farm buildings on the south side of the London Road and opposite to Dunchurch Station, and also a large field to the rear of the buildings. The reason for their use was not disclosed and he was asked to be discreet. On 6th March, a special detachment moved into the farm's brick-built barn and stables, which were whitewashed and painted and the floors scrubbed. When the horses for the royal party subsequently arrived at Dunchurch Station, they were taken to the buildings and groomed, fed and exercised until the day of the inspection. John Mitchell's son, Robert, was only 12 years old at the time but would remember the events clearly:

> "The place was alive with soldiers and horses. There was the clatter of hoofs and hob nailed boots on the cobbles. Tents to sleep in, a mobile kitchen and even their own army vet. Horses were being exercised in the field at the rear (known as Brandy Hole); saddles and harness being cleaned, metal being burnished. Harness chains were tossed repeatedly in a blanket until they shone like silver. The actual stables where the King's horses were being kept were specially guarded. Only those authorised or invited were allowed to enter."[20]

Thus was it ensured that the horses for the royal party were in prime condition for the inspection; proof also that the venue for the inspection had been decided upon some way in advance.

The horse used by the King for the inspection was the famous 'Delhi' and it is 'Delhi' that invariably appears in the photographs that were taken at the time. Although little was published in writing, at least a partial photographic record of the occasion was kept and a number of these pictures would be reproduced as postcards. Most are to do with the King's inspection of the Division on the London Road and show the King making his way

51. *The horses belonging to the royal party about to be loaded onto a wagon at Dunchurch Station; 12th March, 1915.* (© Warwickshire County Record Office)

along the line of review, accompanied not only by his mounted entourage but also by the relevant unit commanding officer, walking by the King's side and answering any questions the King might have about his men. However, there were also a number of amateur shots taken on the day. Some of these relate to the King's Own Scottish Borderers and were taken from the ditch on the south side of the road (see Illustration 48). Another photograph, taken over the heads of some of the crowd, shows what appears to be the Divisional artillery approaching the saluting point, with the King and his entourage to the right. The horses are using the verge of the road (see Illustration 4).

52. *The departure of the King's train; 12th March, 1915.* (© Paul Waller)

Not all of the Division was present on 12th March. In addition to those units, chiefly artillery, that had trained elsewhere, some of the support units were merely 'represented' at the inspection. The 87th Field Ambulance, for example, only provided a stretcher party and an ambulance wagon. These were under the command of Captain Taylor and were located at the Blue Boar Inn; they were there to deal with any emergencies. However, it would seem that they also participated in the march-past. The rest of the men from the 87th Field Ambulance continued their duties in Rugby. During the day, a detail of 15 arrived from the Reserve, to bring the Field Ambulance up to strength, and the men were paid and issued with new boots and clothing.[21] The 89th Field Ambulance, now billeted in Coventry, appear not to have been represented at all. The entry in their war diary for 12th March makes no mention of the inspection, the day being spent in training and in taking delivery of 73 mules from the Remount Depot in Leamington.[22] Those historic events, taking place "in the centre of England where Telford's coaching-road from London to Holyhead is crossed by the Roman Fosse Way", simply passed them by.

 C3

1 The War Diary of the 86th Infantry Brigade Headquarters; National Archives WO95/4310
2 *Rugby Advertiser*, 13th March, 1915
3 *Banbury Guardian*, 11th March, 1915
4 *Banbury Guardian*, 11th March, 1915
5 *Stratford Herald*, 12th March, 1915
6 *Nuneaton Observer*, 12th March, 1915
7 *Nuneaton Observer*, 12th March, 1915
8 *Nuneaton Observer*, 12th March, 1915
9 *Warwick Advertiser*, 13th March, 1915
10 *Nuneaton Observer*, 12th March, 1915
11 *Warwick Advertiser*, 13th March, 1915
12 Letter from Private Edward Aitken, 5th Royal Scots; *Leamington Courier*, 23rd July, 1915. Aitken, in fact, originally came from Leamington.
13 *Coventry Herald*, 19th/20th March, 1915
14 *Nuneaton Observer*, 19th March, 1915
15 *Coventry Herald*, 19th/20th March, 1915
16 Henry Charles Wilkins: "Journal of the Great European War"; Coventry History Centre, JN940.3
17 McConnell, Albert: letter to Peter Liddle, 1977; Liddle Collection, Leeds University Library, GALL (REC) 192. He also recalled the presence at the cross roads of a Boer War veteran, with a short white beard and wearing his medals.
18 *Rugby Advertiser*, 30th January, 1915
19 *Leamington Courier*, 12th March, 1915
20 John Mitchell, unpublished memoir: "A Thurlaston connection with the Review of the newly formed 29th Division at Stretton on Dunsmore on 12th March 1915 by His Majesty King George V"; 1995. Copy held by Stretton on Dunsmore History Society. Brandy Hole is now part of the Whitefield Golf Course. (John Mitchell was the son of Robert Mitchell.)
21 The War Diary of the 87th Field Ambulance Brigade; National Archives WO95/4309
22 The War Diary of the 89th Field Ambulance Brigade; National Archives WO95/4309

12

To Gallipoli

CB

The struggle for the 29th Division

At the soldiers' club at Guy's Dale in Leamington, French lessons were offered by Mrs Benet and Mrs Sovell. These took the form of 'practical French' – such as asking for common necessaries – and did not involve the knowledge of grammar.[1] The YMCA in Rugby also offered lessons in French, which, it was felt, would be of great value when the soldiers "remove to the seat of war".[2] Such classes reflect, of course, the widespread belief that the 29th Division would follow the other regular divisions to the Western Front. Indeed, the Division's training was based upon such an assumption, and Sir John French, Commander-in-Chief of the BEF, was firmly of the opinion that this was the correct use to which the Division – the last intact regular formation – should be put. To this end, he put considerable pressure on Lord Kitchener, Secretary of State for War, whose responsibility it was to deploy the Division. However, in the early weeks of 1915, other plans were being considered and the deployment of the 29th Division became the subject of controversy, though one of which its soldiers were unaware.

On 13th January, 1915, Winston Churchill, First Lord of the Admiralty, had presented a scheme to the War Council for using some of the Royal Navy's older warships to force the Dardanelles Straits, at the eastern end of the Mediterranean. He argued that, if successful, this would enable the Navy to threaten Constantinople, knock Turkey out of the war and bring much-needed help for Britain's ally, Russia. Although Kitchener's initial agreement to the plan was based upon the understanding that no troops would be involved, the question of a military force to accompany the fleet was soon being discussed. The Admiralty argued that troops would be needed to occupy Turkish forts on the Straits and to take part in small-scale landings. On 16th February, Kitchener agreed to send the 29th Division to the Greek island of Lemnos, where it would be available, if required, to support naval operations.

Three days later, on 19th February, the naval bombardment of Turkish forts began. On the same day, Kitchener informed the War Council that he had changed his mind about the 29th Division and that it would now be sent to the Western Front. Churchill's protests were ignored: Kitchener had given in to pressure from Sir John French, who had returned to Britain to argue his case before the War Council. However, even then, the matter was not finally resolved and the Division's fate hung in the balance for more than two weeks. Finally, on 10th March, Kitchener announced that he had decided that the 29th Division would join the Mediterranean Expeditionary Force (MEF). It was considered that the other units available, including the Australian and New Zealand troops completing their training in Egypt, were simply too inexperienced and that regulars were needed to strengthen them.

However, Kitchener still retained doubts, as Sir Ian Hamilton discovered when he was appointed to command the MEF on 12th March, the day of the King's inspection. At his meeting with Kitchener, he was told that "the 29th Division are only to be a loan and are to be returned the moment they can be spared". It was because of this lingering uncertainty on Kitchener's part that the Division was sent to the Mediterranean without the usual 10% draft of reinforcements that accompanied divisions going to the Western Front. It was a decision that the Division would soon have cause to regret.

One further change was the replacement of Major-General F.C. Shaw, as General Officer Commanding the 29th Division, by Major-General Aylmer Hunter-Weston, the announcement being made on 10th March. Shaw appears to have been a popular G.O.C. but his health may not have recovered sufficiently from the wounds he sustained on the Western Front to withstand the rigours of a theatre of war. Hunter-Weston, like Shaw, had commanded a brigade on the Western Front and was brave, energetic and determined. Sir Ian Hamilton described him as "a slashing man of action; an acute theorist", though historians have tended to be less generous. Hunter-Weston was also better known to Kitchener, who may have regarded him as a more dynamic commander. Thus it would be Hunter-Weston's name that went on to the Division's memorial, near Stretton on Dunsmore, even though it was Shaw, in his last duty as G.O.C., who presented the Division to the King on 12th March, 1915.[*]

It was as late as 14th March that senior officers from the 87th Brigade attended a meeting at Brigade Headquarters, at which they were briefed by Hunter-Weston, "who discussed various points bearing on the 29th Division going overseas".[3] However, the decision to send the Division to the Mediterranean had been widely anticipated. Orders had been received at the Divisional Headquarters as early as 24th February that heavy horses should be replaced by mules, the first real indication that the Division might not be sent to the Continent.[4] The 87th Field Ambulance, for example, gave up its horses on 10th March, when they were sent to Leamington, and received a consignment of mules on the 13th. Sun helmets were being issued in early March, by which time there appears to have been a widespread assumption that the Dardanelles was the destination for the Division. On 1st March, Guy Nightingale had told his mother: "We are off to the Dardanelles, I think"[5] and, by 7th March, Oswin Creighton felt it was "obvious" that this was the case.[6] Even a civilian, like the journalist Henry Wilkins, could note in his journal for 15th March that the Division "are said to be going to the Dardanelles", although the move was still an official secret.[7] The Rev. Canon Deed, Vicar of Nuneaton, used his final sermon to the Lancashire Fusiliers (14th March) to remind them that Xerxes realised that the mastery of Europe centred on the possession of Egypt and command of "what is now called the Dardanelles".[8] According to the history of the Worcestershire Regiment, the Army Service Corps drove down to Avonmouth with their lorries carrying signs saying "Cheap trip to the Dardanelles"![9]

Presentations and commendations

The departure of the soldiers was preceded by a flurry of presentations and expressions of mutual appreciation. In Coventry, the Royal Munster Fusiliers received an illuminated scroll of thanks from the city and also a mascot, an 18 month-old, English bull-terrier called

---

[*] Shaw was not long without a command, being appointed G.O.C. of the 13th (Western) Division on 15th March. One of the first New Army divisions, the 13th Division did not go abroad until June, when, somewhat ironically, it was sent to the Gallipoli Peninsula. Shaw's health, however, soon broke down and he was replaced in August by Major-General F.S. Maude. Subsequently, Shaw became Director of Home Defence and then Chief of the General Staff for the Home Forces.

53. *The Royal Munster Fusiliers' mascot, 'Buller', a gift from the people of Earlsdon. His coat was embroidered with the Coventry Arms on one side and the Munsters' Regimental badge on the other. The dog took part in the 'V' Beach landings on 25th April, 1915.* (© Coventry History Centre)

'Buller', which was presented by the inhabitants of Earlsdon. Buller was 'billeted' at a local public house, the City Arms, and was given an overcoat with, appropriately, the Coventry arms on one side and the Munsters' Regimental badge on the other. In Nuneaton, gifts included electric torches, presented to the Royal Fusiliers by the teachers and scholars of Stockingford Council Girls' School. The money had been raised by the sale of work and it was felt that the torches would prove "very valuable in night operations at the front".[10] Soldiers who had attended Nuneaton Wesleyan Church services were presented with a copy each of a New Testament, bound in khaki, as a token of the pleasure that their presence had given members of the Church.[11]

For their part, the soldiers were keen to express their appreciation of the hospitality they had received. Captain F.H. Wilson, Adjutant of the 1st Battalion Royal Munster Fusiliers, spoke of "the many kindnesses given to the regiment during the time the Battalion has been billeted on the city. The men of the Battalion arrived as strangers but thanks to the people of Coventry they now look on the city as a 'home from home.'"[12] Similar sentiments were expressed elsewhere. In Nuneaton, Lieutenant-Colonel Fraser, RAMC, offered a vote of thanks to the townspeople for all they had done for the troops during their stay. In seconding the vote, the Rev. Oswin Creighton expressed particular gratitude to those who had run the recreation rooms. In similar vein, Lieutenant-Colonel R.O.C. Hume expressed the appreciation of all ranks of the Border Regiment for the kindness they had received during their stay in Rugby, especially from those who had run the welcome clubs. The Royal Inniskilling Fusiliers, who had use of the soldiers' club at the Cambridge Street Wesleyan Sunday School, in Rugby, presented Mrs Robotham, "one of the most indefatigable workers", with a solid silver travelling clock, which it was hoped would remind her of the Regiment. In response, Mrs Robotham said that the present was not required to keep their memory fresh, but she would treasure it and never forget the donors.[13]

Those representing the local communities were equally generous in their praise of the departing troops. In Stratford, the Mayor, who also spoke in his capacity as chief magistrate, paid tribute to the excellent conduct of the men of the Hampshire Regiment during their stay in the town: "There was not the slightest cause for complaint in any way."[14] In Leamington, the Mayor said that he thought that the troops billeted there had been so well-behaved that they had actually assisted in policing the town rather than being an obstacle.[15] The Vicar of Nuneaton, the Rev. Canon Deed, told the Lancashire Fusiliers that "you will leave behind you a good name, which is the pride of every regiment".[16] Given the circumstances, such sentiments were perhaps only to be expected but confirmation of the soldiers' general good behaviour comes from a source that was not intended for public consumption. The war diary for the 86th Infantry Brigade Headquarters recorded, in a matter of fact way, that: "The behaviour of the men has on the whole been excellent."[17]

The departure

The departure of the Division from the area began on 15th March, although the real process of leave-taking had already taken place for many of the soldiers at the time of the concentration of the Division about 10 days earlier.

It was originally intended for the troops in Coventry to start leaving on Sunday, 14th March. In the event, their departure was put back 24 hours. Oswin Creighton hoped that he could now use the Sunday to have a church parade for the Royal Fusiliers. However, he was asked not to do so by the Colonel and by the Adjutant, as so many men would be bicycling back to Nuneaton to see their friends and sweethearts, and they would be left with a tremendous list of absentees to punish on the voyage.[18] However, the news of the 24 hour postponement came too late to prevent a crowd of some 3-4,000 assembling in Eaton Road, on the route to the railway station. The crowd included a lot of people from Nuneaton, who had come to Coventry to say farewell to the Royal Fusiliers, many of whom were presumably heading in the opposite direction.[19] The crowds gathered again on Monday and Tuesday (15th and 16th March). Licensed houses were closed from midday on Monday until 2p.m. on Tuesday. The "Tommies" were given "a very hearty send-off",

54. *Royal Munster Fusiliers preparing to leave Coventry; 15th March, 1915.* (© Coventry Graphic)

the parting being "keenly felt on both sides". Large crowds assembled on Pool Meadow to watch the men fall in, while others lined the streets from the top of Hertford Street to Eaton Road. The soldiers were in high spirits and were singing 'Tipperary', and "very few left the city without some little tangible token of esteem".[20]

The departure of the troops from Rugby was also spread over two days. The first contingents left on the afternoon of Tuesday, 16th March; the last in the early hours of Thursday, 18th March. "The troops were given a cheery send-off and many affecting partings were witnessed," according to the *Rugby Advertiser*.[21] The newspaper also noted that: "in many instances a warm affection has sprung up between the soldiers and the residents with whom they were billeted, and to many the parting came as a great wrench". Large crowds accompanied the detachments to the station. The Border Regiment entrained "in the middle of the night" but "even at that hour it seemed that the whole of Rugby had turned out to see them off". By daybreak the next day, the Regiment found itself back at Avonmouth, where it had landed some two months before. The war diary of the 87th Field Ambulance records some of the practicalities of its move from Rugby. Instructions for the departure were issued at the parade at 9.45 a.m. on 17th March. At midnight on the 17th, wagons were sent to the railway station and loaded; the Brigade's animals following at 1.20 a.m. on the 18th. Finally, the men paraded ready for entrainment at 2.00 a.m. and marched to the station 40 minutes later. Their train left Rugby at 3.40 a.m. and arrived at Avonmouth in just under four hours. The weather had turned much colder and it was sleeting as the men boarded their transport ship at 8.30 a.m.

The Lancashire Fusiliers left Nuneaton on three trains in the early hours of Tuesday morning (16th March). On the Monday, notices had been given out that all soldiers must appear on the doorsteps of their billets at 9.25 p.m. to answer their names. They were then instructed to parade on the Battalion parade grounds about two hours before their trains were due to leave. The first train was scheduled to leave at 1.45 a.m. on Tuesday, the others at 4.15 a.m. and 6.45 a.m. In fact, the arrangements worked so smoothly that the trains left earlier than planned. Many local people stayed up throughout the night to see the men off, although the station was closed by the authorities and farewells had to take place in the station yard. In doing so, "the soldiers made sad havoc of the hearts of the gentler sex".[22] Mrs Cole was once again on hand to help dispense refreshments at the station, as she had been when the soldiers first arrived in January. "All the boys quite gloomy over parting", commented Bandsman H. Brown in his diary for 16th March. Four days later, as the transport ship passed Gibraltar, he noted: "Boys still thinking of Nuneaton."[23]

Even in some of the communities where the soldiers had been present for little more than a week, there were similar scenes. It was, perhaps, inevitable that the Royal Dublin Fusiliers appear to have won over the citizens of Kenilworth, as they had those of Torquay and Nuneaton. Despite some initial problems with billeting, they came to be seen as "right good company" and departed on Monday evening (15th March) "with songs and roars of laughter".[24] Two days later, on the evening of Wednesday, 17th March, practically all the villagers of Long Itchington turned out to watch the departure of the 1st West Riding Field Company of the Royal Engineers. After a final hot meal in their billets, the soldiers paraded on the village green at 10.30 p.m. Then, to the accompaniment of "hearty and sincere wishes from the villagers", they marched off into the night on their way to Leamington and an early morning train to Avonmouth.[25] The entrainment of the Worcestershire Regiment at Leamington on 21st March was "a cheerful business", with thousands of the local population joined by "a whole army of relations from Birmingham".[26] By contrast, when 'Y' and 'Z' Companies of the 2nd Battalion Hampshire Regiment had left Warwick, at 3.a.m, on 20th March, the soldiers were told that they must not talk during the march to the station, as their movements were a secret, even though all their billeting hostesses knew exactly what was going on.[27]

The Division's embarkation from Avonmouth took place between 16th and 22nd March.[28] The units travelling from the Midlands were joined at Avonmouth by those that had been in training in other parts of the country. These included the 90th Heavy Battery R.G.A, the 14th Siege Battery R.G.A. and the 1/4th Highland Mountain Brigade, R.G.A., which had only been allocated to the Division on 10th March, the day that Kitchener finally decided to send the 29th Division to join the MEF.[†]

Inevitably, there were some who did not accompany the Division on its departure. About 40 men of the Lancashire Fusiliers, for example, were left behind sick and were due to be sent off later. Apart from a handful of soldiers who were in prison, there also appear to have been a few deserters. On Tuesday, 23rd March, Privates William Kirk and John Green, 1st Battalion Royal Dublin Fusiliers, appeared before Nuneaton Police Court charged with being absent from their regiment: since 8th March, in Kirk's case, and since 2nd February, in Green's. Kirk was arrested in Bedworth, drunk and with the badges on his uniform removed; Green was arrested at the Midland Station in Nuneaton. Green said that he had been in hospital and had returned to Nuneaton not knowing that his Regiment had left; however, his pass was dated 25th January and his story was not believed. Both soldiers were remanded in custody to await a military escort.[29] It should be said that such cases were not uncommon and involved soldiers from many different regiments and not just those associated with the 29th Division. Rather different was the case of Christopher Fitzmaurice, in that he had already been discharged from the 1st Battalion Royal Dublin Fusiliers, for striking an NCO, by the time the Battalion left for Gallipoli. Nearly a year later, in February 1916, he appeared at Nuneaton Law Courts charged with being drunk and disorderly on 20th February and with assaulting two police officers. His behaviour was described as "absolutely mad" and he was sentenced to a month's hard labour at Warwick Prison. Following his discharge from the Army, Fitzmaurice had remained in the area working as a labourer; somewhat unfairly, he was still described by the local paper as "A Dangerous 'Dublin'".[30]

The departure of the soldiers left the communities in which they had been billeted much quieter. In Rugby, "the streets have resumed their ordinary civilian character";[31] in Coventry, "the streets that have been thronged with men in uniform now present a very strange appearance".[32] After the excitement of the soldiers' presence, life began to return to normal. The soldiers' clubs were closed, those who had helped out thanked and the accounts finalised. Places of entertainment were inevitably much quieter, and sport again lapsed. Initially, there were rumours – and hopes – that other troops were to be billeted in the area but these were generally unfounded and nothing on the same scale as the billeting of the 29th Division would occur. In smaller ways as well, normal life resumed. On 22nd March, Amy Wall, of Well Street, in Coventry, appeared before the city magistrates for failing to send her son to school regularly. The boy had been playing truant but explained that he had been following the soldiers. Since their departure, he had attended school regularly and the Bench made an order for this to continue.[33]

☙

[†] However, at least some members of No. 16 Sanitary Section went out in advance of the main party, sailing from Avonmouth on 5th March and arriving at Alexandria on the 14th. (Hammond G.A.: diary; Liddle Collection, Leeds University Library; GALL 042. Hammond was a Sergeant in the Sanitary Corps.)

1. *Leamington Courier*, 22nd January, 1915

2. *Rugby Advertiser*, 6th February, 1915

3. War Diary of the 87th Field Ambulance Brigade; National Archives WO 95/4309

4. War Diary of the 29th Division's Administrative Staff; National Archives WO 95/4306

5. Guy Warneford Papers: National Archives PRO 30/71, letters from Coventry PRO 30/71/3

6. Rev. Oswin Creighton: "With the 29th Division at Gallipoli", Longmans, Green and Co., 1916

7. Henry Wilkins: 'Journal of the Great European War'; Coventry History Centre, JN940.3

8. *Nuneaton Observer*, 19th March, 1915

9. Captain H. FitzM. Stacke: "The Worcestershire Regiment in the Great War"; G.T. Cheshire & Sons Ltd, 1928

10. *Nuneaton Observer*, 19th February, 1915

11. *Nuneaton Observer*, 5th March, 1915

12. *Coventry Herald*, 19th/20th March, 1915

13. *Rugby Advertiser*, 20th March, 1915

14. *Stratford Herald*, 12th March, 1915

15. *Leamington Courier*, 12th March, 1915

16. *Nuneaton Observer*, 12th March, 1915

17. War Diary of the 86th Infantry Brigade Headquarters; National Archives WO 95/4310

18. Rev. Oswin Creighton: op cit

19. *Nuneaton Observer*, 19th March, 1915

20. *Coventry Herald*, 19th/20th March, 1915

21. *Rugby Advertiser*, 20th March, 1915

22. *Nuneaton Chronicle*, 19th March, 1915

23. Brown, H.: diary; Liddle Collection, Leeds University Library, GALL 015

24. *Warwick Advertiser*, 20th March, 1915

25. *Warwick Advertiser*, 20th March, 1915

26. Captain H. FitzM Stacke: op cit

27. Gillett, R.B.: transcript of interview with Peter Liddle, 1973; Liddle Collection, Leeds University Library, GS 0624

28. "History of the Great War: Order of Battle of Divisions, Part 1"; HMSO, 1935. The history of the 29th Division, by Stair Gillon, gives the dates as 15th-19th March.

29. *Nuneaton Observer*, 26th March, 1915

30. *Nuneaton Observer*, 26th February, 1916

31. *Rugby Advertiser*, 20th March, 1915

32. *Coventry Herald*, 19th/20th March, 1915

33. *Coventry Herald*, 26th/27th March, 1915

13

News of the Fighting

ભ

Gallipoli

The 29th Division landed on the Gallipoli Peninsula on 25th April, 1915, some six weeks after the Division had sailed from Avonmouth. Even before the landings, letters were being received in the area from the soldiers, frequently thanking local people for their hospitality. Thus, Drummer J. Burns and Lance Corporal J. Smith wrote in April to thank those who had run the Soldiers' Club at the Friends Meeting House in Rugby for "many happy evenings" that they had spent there.[1] Of 3,000 letters and post cards sent by the 2nd Battalion Hampshire Regiment from the first port of call on the voyage (Malta), 2,500 were addressed to Stratford-upon-Avon.[2] "The number of letters being received in Leamington [from members of the 29th Division] is enormous", stated the *Leamington Courier* for 16th April. The local people were simply not prepared for the volume of letters, mainly from the artillerymen. Members of the 2nd Lowland Field Company wrote from Alexandria to people in Southam to complain about the heat and the fact that they had not been paid since they left the Midlands.[3]

The soldiers were not, of course, at liberty to disclose their destination but one told the *Rugby Advertiser*: "You can tell the people they will hear of us very shortly".[4] Such was the case. The opposed landings on the Peninsula cost the Division dear: approximately a quarter of the Division's rifle strength of 13,000 men were casualties on 25th April. By the time the campaign ended, in January 1915, the Division had suffered 34,011 casualties (killed, wounded, sick or missing), as replacements themselves became casualties. Casualty figures for the three battalions billeted at Nuneaton illustrate the impact of the losses at a regimental level. Of 24 officers and 876 other ranks of the 1st Battalion Royal Dublin Fusiliers who were involved in the landings on 25th April, only one officer and 374 other ranks had <u>not</u> become casualties by the end of April. The strength of the 2nd Battalion Royal Fusiliers on embarkation had been 27 officers and 962 other ranks. By September, only 166 other ranks and not one officer remained unscathed out of their original ranks; in total, the Battalion had suffered, by that point, 279 killed, 954 wounded, 103 missing and some 400 sick. On embarkation, the strength of the 1st Battalion Lancashire Fusiliers had been 26 officers and 932 other ranks; by the end of the campaign, the Battalion had lost 33 officers and 584 other ranks.

News of the casualties

It did not take long for the news of the fighting, and of the casualties being suffered, to filter back to the Warwickshire area. Local newspapers carried the first news of casualties

55. *Lieutenant-Colonel Herbert Carington Smith in Stratford; he was to be remembered for his "kindness, courtesy, chivalry and gentleness".*
(© Shakespeare Birthplace Trust)

on 23rd April, when the losses on the *Manitou* were reported,[*] with 51 feared drowned, including some of "Leamington's Soldier-Guests" who had been billeted with the RFA at Milverton.[5] A full casualty list was published, which also included two members of the 2nd Battalion South Wales Borderers. The news of casualties following the landing on 25th April appeared locally in the week ending 9th May. Predictably, it was the officer casualties that drew the greatest attention. There appears to have been both shock and a genuine sense of loss at the news of Lieutenant-Colonel Herbert Carington Smith's death. He had commanded the 2nd Battalion Hampshire Regiment during its stay in Stratford, where his "kindness, courtesy, chivalry and gentleness" had made him very popular; he was mortally wounded on the bridge of the *River Clyde* during the landings at V Beach.[6] The same landings also claimed the lives of 88th Infantry Brigade's Commanding Officer, Brigadier-

---

[*] On the morning of 17th April, 1915, the transport ship *Manitou*, which was carrying the 147th Brigade RFA from Alexandria, was intercepted by a Turkish torpedo-boat, 10 miles off the island of Skyros. The *Manitou* was sailing without a close escort and the captain of the torpedo-boat ordered the ship to be abandoned immediately, before firing torpedoes. The torpedoes either missed or failed to detonate and the torpedo-boat was driven off by the arrival of British destroyers. However, in the haste to evacuate the ship, some 50 lives were lost, although a greater catastrophe had been narrowly averted.

General Henry E. Napier, and its Brigade-Major, Captain John H.D. Costeker. Napier, who had inspected the Brigade at Radway, was the Division's senior fatality at Gallipoli. Costeker, who had visited Banbury in January to check billeting arrangements, belonged to the Royal Warwickshire Regiment and had been seconded to the Headquarters staff. Lieutenant-Colonel Richard A. Rooth, Commanding Officer of the 1st Battalion Royal Dublin Fusiliers, was another who fell at V Beach.

All three Commanding Officers of the battalions billeted at Rugby were killed. Lieutenant-Colonel Archibald S. Koe (1st King' Own Scottish Borderers) died of wounds on 25th April, following the landing at Y Beach. Lieutenant-Colonel Robert O.C. Hume (1st Border Regiment) was killed on 1st May and Lieutenant-Colonel Francis G. Jones (1st Royal Inniskilling Fusiliers), who had advised the people of Rugby that they could not recover soldiers' debts from their pay, on 5th May. In addition, Lieutenant-Colonel Owen G. Godfrey-Faussett (1st Essex Regiment) fell on the 2nd May. Six out of twelve battalion commanders died in less than two weeks.

Among other well-known figures to be killed was the Rev. Father William Joseph Finn, Chaplain to the 1st Battalion Royal Dublin Fusiliers. According to the *Coventry Herald*, he was the first Catholic chaplain to fall in the war.[7] On 25th April, he had turned down appeals not to get into the landing boats, saying that "the priest's place is beside the dying soldier"; he was shot almost as soon as he set foot ashore. Oswin Creighton subsequently wrote of his death: "The men never forgot him … I think they felt his death almost more than anything that happened in that terrible landing off the *River Clyde*."[8] His loss was also keenly felt among the Catholic community in Kenilworth and a memorial service to him, and to other officers and men from the 1st Battalion Royal Dublin Fusiliers, was held at St Austin's Church on Sunday, 9th May. The service was conducted by Rev. Canon Caswell, with whom Father Finn had stayed during his time in Kenilworth, and a creped portrait of Finn was placed in the porch of the church.[9] Another Dublin whose death touched a particular chord was Major Cecil T.W. Grimshaw, who was killed on 26th April. One of only a handful of officers who had survived the previous day's landings on V Beach, he rallied his men by the unusual expedient of asking: "Do any of you lads want to go back to Nuneaton?" In response, the Dublins present shouted "Aye" and cheered. "Very well, then," said Grimshaw, "make a brilliant charge and may the best men live to return to Nuneaton." With that, he led his men forward. Sadly, Cecil Grimshaw was soon killed but his heroism and his rallying cry, which must surely be unique in the history of the British Army, were understandably appreciated in the town. "How Major Grimshaw Died: Nuneaton Immortalised" was the heading for an article in the *Nuneaton Observer* for 25th June.

Other officer fatalities included Colonel E.P. Smith, Commanding Officer of the 17th Brigade Royal Field Artillery, who was killed on 2nd May. Edmund Smith had become a popular figure in Leamington; he was also the officer whose men had practised at the Deer Park in Stoneleigh and who had befriended Cordelia Leigh's young nephew. 2nd Lieutenant Timothy Sullivan died of wounds on 4th May. Wounded in the thigh by a hand grenade, he was then "bayoneted rather severely".[10] He was 31 years old and had been commissioned from the ranks. His photograph often accompanied the reports of his death, only a few weeks after the publication of the photograph of his wedding to Miss Maud Bates in March. His best man that day, 2nd Lieutenant J. Watts, was wounded at Gallipoli. On 6th May, Captain Thomas Crawley, 4th Battalion Worcestershire Regiment, was killed. He was aged 30 and, in February, as Lieutenant Crawley, he had married Miss Meta Grant; his fiancée had travelled down from Scotland. 2nd Lieutenant Charles Johnson, 1st West Riding Field Company, Royal Engineers, was killed on 6th June. He was remembered in Long Itchington for his courtesy and urbanity when he acted as billeting officer during his Company's brief stay in the village. Among those mourned at Southam was Major William Archibald, Commanding Officer of the 2nd Lowland Field Company, who died of wounds on 18th June. He was 32 years old and was remembered as "a popular officer, although a strict disciplinarian".[11]

56. *Officers of the 1ˢᵗ Battalion Royal Dublin Fusiliers shortly before their departure for Gallipoli; March 1915. Exactly half of the 28 officers shown were killed at Gallipoli. These included, on the front row: Lieutenant-Colonel R.A. Rooth (centre), Captain Cecil Grimshaw (to Rooth's left); on the back row: Lieutenant Henry O'Hara (fifth from left), Rev. Father Finn (ninth from left) and Lieutenant Lawrence Boustead (extreme right).* (© Royal Dublin Fusiliers Association)

Lieutenant Lawrence Boustead, Royal Dublin Fusiliers, was another hero of the break-out from the beaches on 26ᵗʰ April, the action in which Major Grimshaw was killed. Boustead showed great courage and leadership in the capture of the fort at Sedd-el-Bahr. He was wounded in the fighting but subsequently returned to his unit, only to be killed on 29ᵗʰ June. He was 21 years old. During his time in Nuneaton, he had been fined 10s for riding a motorcycle without a light. Lieutenant Henry O'Hara, who was in the same company as Boustead, won the DSO for his part in the landing at 'V' Beach on 25ᵗʰ April. With the other officers in his Battalion having been killed or wounded, he took command of the remnants of the Battalion, displaying great coolness and gallantry. However, he was wounded in action on 12ᵗʰ August and died on the hospital ship *Arcadian*, near Gibraltar, on 29ᵗʰ August. Before attending Charterhouse School, O'Hara had been educated at the preparatory school in Dunchurch, not far from where George V inspected the 29ᵗʰ Division on 12ᵗʰ March. He was 23 years old at the time of his death.

Officer casualties at Gallipoli were appalling, as illustrations 56 and 57 underline. However, the great majority of casualties came from the 'other ranks' and, though they did not always attract the same attention in the local press, their suffering was still keenly felt by those who knew them from the billeting period. In Rugby, there was: "No need to ask when the mails are in. See the girls stop in the streets and the landladies run hatless down to see if there's 'one of their boys' when a train load of wounded comes in."[12] In Leamington, "There will be hundreds of ... people keeping a sharp eye on the papers for names."[13] By the beginning of June, the *Nuneaton Observer* was publishing extensive lists of killed and wounded for the battalions that had been billeted in the town, with several hundred names of "Nuneaton's Soldier Friends".

Fatalities included men who had become well-known in Rugby, such as Serjeant James Johnston, of the Border Regiment, whose involvement in the Rugby Baptist Church is described in Section 8. He was killed in action on the opening day of the campaign, 25ᵗʰ April. Lance Corporal Joseph Giles, also of the Border Regiment, was killed on 11ᵗʰ June. Born in Kidderminster in 1887, he was living with his parents in Coventry when he enlisted in the Border Regiment in the summer of 1906. He spent his army service overseas, with two years at Gibraltar and six years in India and Burma. He played hockey, Association football

57. *Officers of the 1ˢᵗ Battalion Border Regiment; Rugby, February 1915. Of the 25 officers pictured, only two did not become casualties at Gallipoli. Lieutenant-Colonel R.O.C. Hume (middle of front row) was one of 10 who were killed in action or died of wounds. Captain F.H.S. Le Mesurier (see Page 16) is on the extreme left, front row, and Major G. Brooke (see Page 132) is third from the right, front row.* (© Cumbria Military Museum)

and was a member of the Battalion tug of war team. He also played the euphonium in the Regimental band. He was remembered in Rugby as "a fine all round sportsman"; however, to Corporal E.F. Hancox, who communicated the news of his death to their former billets in Railway Terrace, Giles was simply "my best chum".[14] On 1ˢᵗ January, 1916, Sergeant James Meneilly, Royal Inniskilling Fusiliers, died of wounds on a hospital ship and was buried at sea. Billeted in Cambridge Street, 'Corporal Jim' had become involved in the Cambridge Street Wesleyan Soldiers' Home, where his rich voice meant he had been much in demand as a singer.[15] In March 1916, an unnamed bandsmen reported that he was "the only one left with the Regiment out of the band we had in Rugby", and which used to play in Caldecott Park.[16]

Among those billeted at Banbury who subsequently died at Gallipoli was Company Sergeant Major Bernard Steven, the "very epitome of the soldier of Empire" (see Page 25). He was killed on 4ᵗʰ June, when the 1ˢᵗ Battalion Essex Regiment was brought forward from Brigade Reserve to participate in the third attack on the village of Krithia. He was shot twice, according to Private Sydney White in a letter home. Bernard Steven has no known grave and is commemorated on the Helles Memorial. He left a wife and three children, the youngest of whom he had never seen. Fatalities among those billeted at Nuneaton included Private Charles Hutchinson, 1ˢᵗ Battalion Royal Dublin Fusiliers, whose father had been involved in the traffic accident whilst visiting his son in January; Charles died of wounds on 29ᵗʰ June.

In Coventry, those reported killed included Sergeant William O'Hanlon, 1ˢᵗ Battalion Royal Munster Fusiliers. He was 27 years old and considered the finest athlete in the Battalion, the winner of many medals for his sporting achievements and captain of the Regimental football and hockey teams. During his time in Coventry, he had frequently acted as referee at the Earlsdon Ladies' Hockey Club matches. He was killed in action on 25ᵗʰ April. Sergeant Drummer Joseph Hickey was killed in action on 1ˢᵗ May. In time of war, bandsmen became stretcher bearers and Hickey was killed while attending a wounded comrade. He is shown at the head of the band pictured on Page 66, as the Fusiliers marched to church in Coventry. Another popular Munster Fusilier who died was Pioneer-Sergeant Robert Ireland who was well-known among local Good Templars; he was killed when a dug-out collapsed upon him on 12th May. George Bunce of the 2nd Battalion South Wales Borderers had been another well-liked figure. A Sergeant when he arrived in Coventry, his subsequent promotion to 2nd Lieutenant gave considerable satisfaction. It was said that, when he received notification of his promotion, he was cleaning a comrade's buttons and finished the task. He was killed in action on 12th May and left a wife and child.[17]

Sometimes it was little more than "poor old Tim [or 'Spider' or 'Fussy' or 'Smiler' etc] has been killed". In a letter written from hospital, Private G. Heywood, 1st Battalion Lancashire Fusiliers, brought his former landlady, Mrs Norris, of Weddington Lane, Nuneaton, up to date:

"I have not heard anything of Magill. Nobody seems to know anything about him at all. We have lost all our officers now, except the youngest one of the lot, and from the talk you hear from the fresh wounded, there is hardly any N.C.O.s and men left. One of my chums has got the Distinguished Conduct Medal. He was billeted at Mr Smith's (the builder in Wheat Street). ... The two lads who were billeted at Mr Cave's have been killed. Mr Cooper's lads, one has been killed and the other wounded. Ducket's had one killed and one wounded, but as regard to Peabody's I know absolutely nothing."[18]

Private Heywood concluded nostalgically: "I bet it is grand round Warwickshire now the fine weather has come."

Sometimes the uncertainty that could surround reports of casualties can be glimpsed. The *Stratford Herald* for 23rd July, 1915, published a statement from Lance Corporal W.C.J.E. Robinson, 2nd Battalion Hampshire Regiment, to say that he had not been killed on 25th April, as rumoured, although he had been wounded on 4th June. However, he was now ready for active service again. (He was killed a year later, on 9th August, 1916, during a phosgene gas attack at Potijze, in Belgium.) The *Rugby Advertiser* for 21st August carried an appeal from Mr James Hewson, a mason from Harrington, in Cumberland, for news of his son Corporal Jonathan Hewson, 1st Battalion Border Regiment, who had been reported missing since 9th May. Mr A. Bird, Claremont Road, Rugby, had offered his services to gather information from wounded officers and soldiers, as well as from those at the front. It is not known when the news of Sergeant (as he had become) Jonathan Hewson's death finally reached his family but the delay could sometimes be several months. The date of death would be given as 9th May.

Equally touching is a letter from Mrs Jennings, from Swansea, who wrote to thank the people of Coventry for the kind reception they had given the 2nd Battalion South Wales Borderers, in which two of her sons had been serving. Sadly, Corporal John Jennings had died of wounds on 19th May; his brother Willie had been wounded shortly before. The two brothers had fought practically side by side. Of 18 members of the extended family serving with the forces, John was the fifth to fall.[19]

There was somewhat better news of 'Buller', the dog presented to the Royal Munster Fusiliers. In a letter to Mr Williamson, of Earlsdon, in Coventry, Private Daniel Murphy explained what had happened to the dog:

"The poor old dog landed all right [at V Beach on 25th April], but rushed back to the boat again, and stopped there till I went there two days later. He was very frightened. Well, it would frighten any dog, the landing under shrapnel fire and rifle fire. So he is on board a battleship now, and they are looking after him till we reach Constantinople."

Private Murphy expressed the intention of returning 'Buller' at the end of the war, "that is if any of us are alive to fetch him back". His melancholy was shared by others who had survived the initial fighting and who had seen the numbers of those who had sailed from England dwindle. In August, Private Griffiths, 2nd Battalion South Wales Borderers, probably summed up the feelings of many when he concluded his account of the fighting, and the losses to the original Battalion, by saying: "It is like a new regiment."[20]

Accounts of the fighting

Some of the letters passed on to the local newspapers for publication contained graphic accounts of the fighting at Gallipoli. Not surprisingly, it was the descriptions of the landings that were initially prominent:

> "The first two boat-loads from the ship were swept by a murderous machine gun and sniping fire from the shore and I do not think a man escaped."[21]

> "It was like a hailstorm of bullets. There are only about 200 of our battalion left. It was hell on earth. ... We landed in small boats – or tried to. There were 35 in my boat and seven sailors. Only another sergeant and myself got out of it. The others were killed in the boat and then it was set on fire. Never mind. We are doing great work."[22]

> "We lost a terrible lot of men when we first went into action. ... It was awful: what with the groans of the wounded and the men being drowned. ... I was beside my cousin when he got his head blown off his shoulders. The young man who stopped next door but one to you, at 132, got the bottom part of his jaw shot away."[23]

Under the headline: "Landing of the Border Regiment in the Dardanelles. Knocked over in hundreds", appeared an account by Corporal White. Like many of the other correspondents, White was among those who had been wounded and who wrote back to his friends from hospital or, in his case, hospital ship:

> "We landed on Sunday, and had to climb a big cliff before we got to level ground, and as we came over this cliff the enemy were firing on us. Of course, they were knocking our men over in hundreds, as we were in the open and they were in trenches only about 200 yards away. ... My officer got killed before he had gone twenty yards."[24]

A week later, a letter from an officer in the Border Regiment was published in the *Rugby Advertiser* under the heading "Heavy Losses of 29th Division in Dardanelles." The officer also left little doubt as to the nature of the fighting:

> "Our losses, I am sorry to say have been terrible. ... The Turks are fighting fiercely. ... The naval guns are useless against land forces."[25]

In the same edition of the newspaper, Private Albert Holbrook, of the King's Own Scottish Borderers, was quoted as saying: "we have had a hard time of it since we arrived".[26] In Coventry, it was reported that: "The poor Munsters got a great wiping out"[27] and that: "We have been 'through it' since I last wrote."[28] "It wasn't a picnic" was a more understated comment from a member of the 5th Battalion Royal Scots, writing to a friend in Leamington.[29] Even a letter that appeared in the *Banbury Advertiser* under the heading "Cheery Letter from an Essex Soldier" included: "the Turks simply mowed us down".[30] By the end of August, accounts were appearing under the heading: "Letters from the Remnants of the 29th Division".[31]

Munsters' and S.W.B. Borderers' Casualties.

1, Pte. G. Skinner, R.M F. (killed) ; 2, Pte. G. Steaney. S W.B. (killed) ; 3, Sergt. Rogers, S.W B. (killed) ; 4, Pte. C. Waters, S.W B. (killed); 5, Drummer W. Jones, S W.B. (killed) ; 6, Sergt. A. W. Jones, S.W.B. (killed) ; 7, Pte. Harrad. S.W.B. (wounded) ; 8, Corpl. Cheesman, S.W.B. (killed) ; 9, Pte. E. Jones, S.W.B. (wounded) ; 10, Pte. W. Cusick, S.W B. (killed) ; 11, Pte. T. O'Connell. S W B. (died of wounds).

58. *The lengthy casualty lists and photographs appearing in the newspapers in 1915 can have left local people with few illusions as to the losses suffered by the 29th Division at Gallipoli;* Coventry Graphic, *17th September, 1915.* (© Coventry Graphic)

People in the Warwickshire area can have had few illusions about what had happened to the units billeted upon them. On 7th June, 1916, Henry Wilkins recorded in his Journal:

> "Went to Stretton on Dunsmore, and to the spot where his Majesty the King inspected the 29th Division in March 1915. Wonder how many of these thousands of men are still in the field? Not many, I fear."[32]

Comforts for the troops

Amidst the dramatic news of the fighting and of the losses being suffered at Gallipoli, contacts between the billeting area and the 29th Division also continued at a more mundane level. It seems the soldiers felt rather left out of things in terms of the provision of comforts, a situation exacerbated by the authorities who were slow to send out parcels, many of which appear to have gone astray. Lieutenant F.D. Silk, 2nd Battalion Hampshire Regiment, writing to a friend in Stratford, thought that those at Gallipoli had neither the comforts nor the attention of "the fellows" in France, and yet were doing harder and more uncomfortable work.[33][†] Not surprisingly, many looked to their friends in the billeting area for assistance and there was a steady flow of requests for socks, cigarettes ("especially Woodbines"), writing pads, pencils and other comforts, as well as a hair cutting outfit ("we are fed up here with long hair"), an old violin and a B flat clarinet. The area responded to these appeals, as it did to similar appeals made by local soldiers. In November, for example, as a result of a series of dances held at the Salisbury Hall, in Leamington, several parcels were sent out to some of the units in the 29th Division. The parcels contained shirts, scarves, socks, mittens, biscuits, cocoa, soup tablets, soap etc.[34]

[†]   However, Silk also felt that the 29th Division suffered from being the only regular division and "consequently have all the dirty work to do in the way of having to clean up the mess and keep the show going".

Whether fly-paper counted as a comfort is debateable but one artilleryman, no doubt facetiously, suggested that "the sooner the British people send out some fly-papers the better. … Someone had better start a 'Fly-paper Fund', for they have started almost every other fund." A fellow artilleryman said of the flies at Gallipoli: "The place is black with them. If one tries to eat anything it is always accompanied as far as one's mouth by a horde of flies that hang on like grim death."[35] At Banbury, a request was received, in June, from the Essex Regiment for funds with which to purchase x-ray apparatus, the existing machine being insufficient to help deal with the large numbers of wounded. By October, the townspeople were being thanked for having raised the money (£133), with the apparatus now in constant use at a hospital in Alexandria.[36] Among souvenirs returning from the Dardanelles were "two shells" (presumably shell cases), weighing 6 ½ lbs. These were received by Mr and Mrs Aitken, New Street, Leamington; their benefactor was their son, Private A.W. Aitken, of the Army Ordnance Corps attached to the 29th Division.[37]

Returning Soldiers

Some of the wounded who had been sent back to the United Kingdom had the opportunity to visit the billeting area. In other cases, local people visited the wounded in British hospitals: in May, for example, a group from Rugby journeyed to a hospital near Manchester. The accounts of the fighting told by the wounded simply confirmed the impressions already formed. In late May, "a well-known Sergeant in the Royal Dublin Fusiliers", who had been

billeted in Norman Avenue, Nuneaton, paid a brief visit to the town, during which time he was interviewed by a representative of the *Nuneaton Observer*. He had been wounded on 25th April and gave a detailed account of the landing, which appeared under the heading "To Death or Glory". "The flower of the famous 1st Dublins were either killed, drowned or wounded without having the chance to defend themselves", although those who did get ashore "fought in magnificent fashion to avenge their fallen comrades".[38] Another Dublin Fusilier who visited Kenilworth on 27th May claimed that six men from 'D' Company had been burned alive by the Turks. The story, which appeared under the heading "Dublin Fusiliers Tortured", was repeated in other local newspapers.[39] Those returning to Rugby included Private Harris, of the Border Regiment, who had been billeted in Craven Road, and who described the fighting as "simply terrible".[40] In a 'chat' with a reporter from the *Advertiser*, Private Bonner, of the Royal Inniskilling Fusiliers, who had stayed in Abbey Street, said that men had been "mown down" in their hundreds but had never flinched.[41]

59. *Private J.M. Meers, Royal Munster Fusiliers, on his return to Coventry in August 1915. Meers went back to his former billet in Sovereign Road, Earlsdon, to recuperate from wounds caused by two bullets and a bayonet.* (© Coventry Graphic)

In July, two badly-wounded Dublins were invited to stay in Kenilworth. Privates Walsh and Devlin, each of whom had lost a leg, were invited to recuperate at homes in the town, the *Warwick Advertiser* commenting that "even now there are Kenilworth people anxious to do their bit for the heroes of the 'V' beach landing".[42] In August, similar offers from Kenilworth were made to three other wounded Dublins: Private Whelan, who had also lost a leg, Private Griffin, who "would find a comfortable home waiting for him at the house of Mrs Garlick", and an unnamed soldier, albeit one from whom no news had been received for a long while. Given the brevity of the Dublins' stay in Kenilworth, such offers say a good deal about the generosity of people there.

Such was the attraction of the former billeting area that some soldiers came back whether they had permission or not. Private William Hawkins, 1st Battalion Dublin Fusiliers, appeared at Nuneaton Police Court on 5th October charged with being a deserter from Rubery Hill Military Hospital, Birmingham. He had come to Nuneaton on the previous Sunday, still dressed in his hospital clothes. He was ordered to await an escort to accompany him back to Birmingham.[43] In November, two Lancashire Fusiliers, who had overstayed their leave in Nuneaton, also ended up in the police cells. They had both been involved in the landings at the Dardanelles and appear not to have been unduly daunted by their new circumstances, their vocal powers earning them the nickname "the two Lancashire nightingales". During their appearance at the Nuneaton Police Court, "the deep-throated melody of the Lancashire heroes was repeatedly heard".[44]

଒

[1]   *Rugby Advertiser*, 25th April, 1915
[2]   *Stratford Herald*, 21st May, 1915
[3]   *Leamington Courier*, 22nd April, 1915
[4]   *Rugby Advertiser*, 10th April, 1915
[5]   *Leamington Courier*, 23rd April, 1915
[6]   *Stratford Herald*, 7th May, 1915. N.B.: Carington is frequently spelt Carrington; for example, on the monument to the 29th Division.
[7]   *Coventry Herald*, 14th/15th May, 1915
[8]   Rev. Oswin Creighton: "With the 29th Division at Gallipoli", Longmans, Green and Co., 1916
[9]   *Coventry Herald*, 14th/15th May, 1915
[10]   *Nuneaton Observer*, 27th August, 1915
[11]   *Leamington Courier*, 2nd July, 1915
[12]   *Rugby Advertiser*, 5th June, 1915
[13]   *Warwick Advertiser*, 5th June, 1915
[14]   *Rugby Advertiser*, 17th July, 1915
[15]   *Rugby Advertiser*, 29th January, 1916
[16]   *Rugby Advertiser*, 11th March, 1916
[17]   *Coventry Graphic*, 21st May, 1915
[18]   *Nuneaton Observer*, 25th June, 1915
[19]   *Coventry Herald*, 18th/19th June, 1915
[20]   *Rugby Advertiser*, 7th August, 1915
[21]   Letter from Private E. Carrell, 2nd Battalion Hampshire Regiment: *Stratford Herald*, 14th May, 1915
[22]   Letter from unnamed sergeant in the 1st Battalion Royal Dublin Fusiliers; *Nuneaton Observer*, 14th May, 1915
[23]   Extract from letter by Private J. Ellis, 1st Battalion Lancashire Fusiliers; *Nuneaton Observer*, 14th May, 1915
[24]   *Rugby Advertiser*, 22nd May, 1915
[25]   *Rugby Advertiser*, 29th May, 1915
[26]   *Rugby Advertiser*, 29th May, 1915
[27]   Private Dennesley; quoted in the *Coventry Herald*, 28th/29th May, 1915
[28]   Sergeant John Sheehan, 1st Battalion Royal Munster Fusiliers; *Coventry Herald*, 11th/12th June, 1915
[29]   *Warwick Advertiser*, 26th June, 1915

30 *Banbury Advertiser*, 19th August, 1915: letter from Private F. Taylor to Mr F. Cripps, custodian of the Banbury Conservative Club

31 *Rugby Advertiser*, 28th August, 1915

32 Henry Charles Wilkins: "Journal of the Great European War"; Coventry History Centre, JN940.3

33 *Stratford Herald*, 23rd July, 1915

34 *Leamington Courier*, 19th November, 1915

35 From letters in the *Leamington Courier*, 6th August, 1915

36 *Banbury Guardian*, 10th June and 21st October, 1915

37 *Leamington Courier*, 20th August, 1915

38 *Nuneaton Observer*, 28th May, 1915

39 *Leamington Courier*, 28th May, 1915

40 *Rugby Advertiser*, 22nd May, 1915

41 *Rugby Advertiser*, 29th May, 1915

43 *Warwick Advertiser*, 10th July, 1915

43 *Nuneaton Observer*, 8th October, 1915

44 *Nuneaton Observer*, 3rd December, 1915

14

"The Incomparable 29th"

☙

"Fond memories"

Local newspapers were, of course, always willing to publish the numerous compliments subsequently paid by the 29th Division's soldiers to local communities. Corporal W.J. Northam, 1st Battalion Royal Inniskilling Fusiliers, found it "a terrible struggle to leave Rugby and the people who treated us so kindly". Although they were only in Rugby for nine weeks, "we were treated much more like relatives than strange soldiers".[1] Lance Corporal A.J. Smith, 1st Border Regiment, said that he and his comrades often sat in the trenches, "waiting to pop off Turks", whilst recalling "fond memories of dear old Rugby and the Bilton Road especially".[2] Some of the trenches and dug-outs at Gallipoli were even named after places in Rugby, such as 'Worcester Square' and 'Wood Street Cave'.[3]

Soldiers billeted elsewhere were just as complimentary. Five soldiers from the 2nd Battalion Royal Fusiliers, writing on behalf of themselves "and all the other rabbits in the adjoining burrows", remembered how "we were always made at home wherever we went. ... The boys are continually talking about the good times they had, and the password in the trenches is 'Roll on Stocko and Nuno'. They tell us we shall be coming back soon, so please keep our beds aired ..."[4] To Sergeant Grimshaw, 1st Battalion Lancashire Fusiliers, his stay in Nuneaton was "about the happiest time in my life".[5] Sergeant Byrne of the Royal Dublin Fusiliers felt "the people of Nuneaton ... treated us better than some of us would expect of our home".[6] "How I would like to be in dear old Banbury, with our good old landlady (Mrs Herbert of Grove St) and then go to the Conservative Club", wrote Private F. Taylor, 1st Battalion Essex Regiment. Private O'Brien, 1st Battalion Royal Munster Fusiliers, said of Coventry: "I never met a nicer lot in all my time, no matter where I travelled."[7]

No doubt the privations of Gallipoli, coming so soon after the comforts of billeting, encouraged nostalgia:

"Who of the battalion [5th Royal Scots] will ever forget Leamington, the pleasant route marches into the delightful countryside, the days of comfort under practically home conditions ... amongst inhabitants who treated the men with great kindness? What halcyon nights there were with the bagpipes playing and dancing with the village [sic] maidens by the lamplight."[8]

The 29th Division's growing reputation

The landings, the intense fighting that followed and the heavy losses inevitably helped build the reputation of the Division. Hunter-Weston's personal note "to each man of the 29th Division on the occasion of their first going into action together" was widely quoted in the local newspapers: "The eyes of the world are upon us, and your deeds will live in history." Praise for individual battalions was also passed on to the billeting area, such as Hunter-Weston's "Well done the Dubs!"*, on their relief from the firing line after 15 days continuous fighting, and his generous tribute to the Hampshires: "You have achieved the impossible." By the end of June, Sir Ian Hamilton was referring to "the incomparable 29th Division". In November, an article by the British war correspondent Ellis Ashmead-Bartlett was reproduced in the *Warwick Advertiser*. Ashmead-Bartlett wrote of the 29th Division's "Homeric struggle in the Dardanelles" and was another who compared the survivors of the original division to Napoleon's Old Guard. He also remarked upon the way in which the young and inexperienced drafts of replacements absorbed the traditions of the Division and invariably distinguished themselves – such was the "mysterious halo" of "No. 29". Thus did the Division's reputation become established, no doubt encouraged by the fact, as Ashmead-Bartlett pointed out, that all four countries that made up the United Kingdom were represented in its ranks and could identify with its achievements.[9]

Among the many awards won by soldiers from the Division at Gallipoli were 12 VCs and particular pride was taken in the communities in which the VC winners had been billeted, not least Nuneaton, which had hosted the 1st Battalion Lancashire Fusiliers, winners of the "Six VCs Before Breakfast" during the landing at W beach on 25th April.[†] Corporal William Cosgrove, 1st Battalion Royal Munster Fusiliers, had been billeted in the Earlsdon part of Coventry and won a VC for his actions on 26th April. "The hero is well-known in Coventry."[10] 2nd Lieutenant G. R. Dallas Moor of the 2nd Battalion Hampshire Regiment, which had been billeted in Stratford and in Warwick, became the youngest VC winner in the Mediterranean Expeditionary Force for his actions on 6th June. The 18 year-old halted a disorganised retreat of men from other units by the drastic expedient of shooting one or two of the fugitives, before leading a successful counter-attack. Lieutenant Herbert James, 4th Battalion Worcestershire Regiment, who had been billeted in Banbury and Leamington, won his VC for his bravery between 28th June and 2nd July.

However, perhaps the closest association between a locality and a VC winner was that between Rugby and Sergeant James Somers, 1st Battalion Royal Inniskilling Fusiliers. Whilst still holding the rank of corporal, Somers was awarded the Division's twelfth VC for his actions on the night of 1st-2nd July 1915.[‡] He returned to Rugby on 14th October, 1915, when he received a "remarkable ovation". He was met at the railway station by Mr J.J. McKinnell, leader of the Council, and Colonel Johnstone, recruiting officer for Rugby, along with a crowd of several thousand. His journey through the town was made in a landau, "drawn by a number of stalwart admirers". He returned to Corbett Street, where he had been billeted with Mr and Mrs William Burn. A small, decorated arch had been erected outside the house, with the legend "Welcome VC", and Mrs Burn presented James Somers with a wrist watch. An estimated 10,000 townspeople turned out to do Somers honour and a band played "See The Conquering Hero Comes". Before departing for his home in Ireland, Somers addressed a recruiting rally in Rugby. However, despite the large numbers

---

*   Alternatively, "Well done Blue Caps!"

†   However, three of these VCs were not awarded until March 1917; the others had been gazetted in August 1915.

‡   However, Captain Gerald O'Sullivan, 1st Battalion Royal Inniskilling Fusiliers, who had also been billeted in Rugby, who was involved in the same action as Somers on 1st-2nd July, and whose VC was announced on the same day as that of Somers, does not appear to have attracted the same attention in Rugby. In part, this may have been because O'Sullivan was subsequently killed in the fighting at Gallipoli in August and could not make a triumphal return. The other VC winner from the Division in the fighting at Gallipoli was Captain Garth Neville Walford, Brigade-Major Royal Artillery, who was awarded a posthumous VC for his actions on 26th April, the same fighting as claimed the life of Cecil Grimshaw.

60. *James Somers, 1ˢᵗ Battalion Royal Inniskilling Fusiliers, who was billeted with Mr and Mrs William Burn, Corbett Street, Rugby. He won his VC at Gallipoli in July 1915, whilst still a corporal. He received a hero's welcome when he visited Rugby in October 1915.* (© Warwickshire Library and Information Service)

in attendance, the "manly appeal" from Somers appears to have had little effect: a week later a letter from him was published in the local paper, thanking the townspeople for their reception whilst expressing disappointment at the lack of fresh recruits.[11]

Other acts of heroism that were publicised included those of two Munster Fusiliers, Privates J. Slattery and M. Twomey, who rescued two surviving horses from a Divisional Signalling Cart. This involved dashing some 300 yards, "in a hail of shellfire" to bring the horses to safety, even though men from other units "were unable to move out of their trenches within 20 yards of the scene". The incident was described in a letter from Lieutenant Guy Nightingale.[12]

"Our soldiers"

So close was the identification of the area with the men who had been billeted there that it became common practice to refer to them as "our soldiers" or "our boys". Leamington, indeed, went one step further and described the 29ᵗʰ Division as "the Leamington Division", citing "the men of the 29ᵗʰ", who had come to regard themselves in that way.[13] The *Nuneaton Observer*, in writing about the casualty lists, said that: "Many Nuneaton folk feel that they have lost one of their own family."[14]

In an "open letter to our soldiers", published in the *Rugby Advertiser* on 5ᵗʰ June, "several of your old landladies" spoke of the widespread concern for the welfare of their "dear boys" and it had already become commonplace in the paper to publish news of "Our Soldiers in the Dardanelles". Not surprisingly, some of those soldiers who actually did come from Rugby felt as though they were being overlooked. In a 'Remonstrance from the Trenches' (also published in the *Advertiser* on 5th June), members of 'E' Company of the 7th Battalion Royal Warwickshire Regiment, containing many of Rugby's Territorial soldiers, complained of the preference being given to the soldiers billeted in the town over the men of the local forces: "Rugby men seem to have been forgotten since 'Our Soldiers' were at Rugby." The following week, the Editor of the *Advertiser* considered it necessary to offer "An Explanation" of the town's feelings, together with an assurance that the town's sentiments towards its Territorial soldiers had not changed. "Rugby people have not forgotten that they have a strong and gallant contingent of fellow-townsmen bravely representing them and upholding the honour of the country at the front."[15]

Within the Division there were those who felt that disproportionate attention was being paid to the infantry. Driver Biddle, RAMC, noted articles in the *Rugby Advertiser* about all the regiments in Rugby except the RAMC. "I wonder why this is because in our own work we have done equally as much as any of the infantry regiments. ... I think we must be like the Navy. We do our duty silently, but nevertheless efficiently."[16] If nothing else, such correspondence shows the extent to which local newspapers were circulating among soldiers at Gallipoli, on the Western Front and in the training areas in the United Kingdom.

A proposed Fusiliers' memorial in Nuneaton

Matters became even more heated in Nuneaton, following the proposal for a memorial to the Fusiliers who had been billeted in the town. At the beginning of August, the *Nuneaton Observer* suggested that the fate of the "Gallant Twenty-Ninth" ought to call forth a fitting memorial in the borough. The newspaper was of the opinion that Nuneaton's inhabitants would "support such a memorial handsomely".[17] Whatever the views of Nuneaton's civilians, the idea provoked considerable indignation among local soldiers. A letter from 13 "Nuneaton lads" in 'D' Company, 1st Battalion Royal Warwickshire Regiment, pointed out that the Fusiliers "were only in the town for 8 weeks" and yet "it seems they were worshipped in Nuneaton as some superior beings, and are mentioned in the newspapers week after week". It was felt that the money ought to be put to "a memorial of our own" – to the local men who had died, from all regiments and not just the county regiment.[18] The first name at the end of the letter was that of Private J. Jauncey; along with three other signatories, Jauncey died later in the war and his name can be found on the town's war memorial in Riversley Park.

The debate about the proposed Nuneaton memorial rumbled on for several months, with letters, usually in opposition to the idea, appearing at regular intervals, from "somewhere in the fighting line", or "a few words from the trenches" etc. The basic arguments were the same: "our own brave lads who have died for their country should be considered first"; "from what I can see, the Nuneaton people don't give a -- for their own County Regiment"; "our Division was billeted in Surrey for twelve weeks. What would the people of that county think if they considered us first and not their own lads"; "the townspeople think a lot more of strangers than they do of their own kinsmen", and so on. A local soldier, Private G. Twigger, was at home wounded when the Fusiliers were in Nuneaton and found them "a very quiet lot of fellows". He thought that they had done good work at the Dardanelles but he did not favour a memorial: "The Fusiliers were not formed in Nuneaton, only billeted there."[19]

The surviving members of the Fusiliers' Brigade no doubt had other things to worry about than memorials but, when they did respond, it was usually in a diplomatic manner: "It is only right that the Warwicks should come first. The only memorial we want is the lasting goodwill of Nuneaton people."[20] The proposed memorial would not come at the expense of one to local men but "simply shows the sympathy and love the people of Nuneaton wish to

Fusiliers at Nuneaton:

61. *Members of the 2ⁿᵈ Battalion Royal Fusiliers outside the Conservative Club, Stockingford.* (© David Fordham)

62. *Royal Dublin Fusiliers and civilian friends.* (© Warwickshire County Record Office)

show those who were once billeted with them and who cared for us as if they were their own sons."[21] One of the Dublins wrote to express the sympathy the Dublins felt for the victims of the Exhall mining disaster in September, when 14 local miners lost their lives. However, Bandsman Hartman, of the Royal Fusiliers, couldn't understand "what the fuss is about – a memorial to the Fusiliers would not be at the expense of one to local men".

It was the "Protest of Eight Nuneaton Lads", who felt the work of the 11th Division at Gallipoli was equally illustrious, that provoked a more vigorous response. Six soldiers, representing five different regiments in the 29th Division, suggested that the Eight should take a look at Sir Ian Hamiliton's report on the 29th Division's part in the landings in April, and the 18 days' continuous fighting that followed. They also hoped that the "selfishness" of the writers and of "the Warwickshire fighting men will no more be shown towards the Fusiliers' Brigade or the famous 29th Division". However, "whether a memorial is created or not, we send the highest praise and goodwill to the people of Nuneaton for the kindness showed to the men of the 86th Fusiliers' Brigade".[22]

In the midst of this debate, Betty Fennell paid her own heartfelt homage to some of the billeted soldiers, in the form of a poem, which appeared under the title "A Hurrah for the 2nd Royal Fusiliers":

"Hurrah for the gallant Royals: plucky little men.
I am thinking hard about them, as the ink rolls off my pen.
For never since the day, when first the Royals 'took the kiss';
Could the regiment boast a prouder, or nobler deed than this."

... and so forth for another seven verses. Betty called herself "the Dood Wallah" and she came from Queen's Road Farm in Nuneaton. A "dood wallah" was army slang for a milkman and originated among the troops in India.[23]

In the end, there would be no memorial in Nuneaton for the Fusiliers' Brigade. However, when the post-war memorial to the 29th Division was erected near Stretton on Dunsmore, the article in the *Nuneaton Observer* appeared under the heading "Nuneaton's Billeted Soldiers. Splendid Memorial."[24] The same newspaper perhaps struck the right note when the memorial was unveiled in May 1921, when it was described as "Warwickshire's Tribute to Her Adopted Sons".[25]

ॐ

1   *Rugby Advertiser*, 29th May, 1915
2   *Rugby Advertiser*, 17th July, 1915
3   *Rugby Advertiser*, 28th August, 1915
4   *Nuneaton Observer*, 4th June, 1915
5   Letter published in *Nuneaton Observer*, 6th August, 1915
6   *Nuneaton Observer*, 8th October, 1915
7   *Coventry Herald*, 16th/17th July, 1915
8   Article in an Edinburgh newspaper quoted in the *Leamington Courier*, 16th July, 1915
9   *Warwick Advertiser*, 6th November, 1915
10   *Coventry Herald*, 27th/28th August, 1915
11   *Rugby Advertiser*, 16th and 23rd October, 1915
12   *Coventry Herald*, 2nd/3rd July, 1915
13   *Leamington Courier*, 23rd July, 1915
14   *Nuneaton Observer*, 7th May, 1915
15   *Rugby Advertiser*, 12th June, 1915
16   *Rugby Advertiser*, 28th August, 1915
17   *Nuneaton Observer*, 6th August, 1915
18   *Nuneaton Observer*, 20th August, 1915.
19   *Nuneaton Observer*, November 5th, 1915
20   Letter from Horace Hodkinson, 1st Battalion Lancashire Fusiliers, *Nuneaton Observer*, 24th September, 1915.
21   *Nuneaton Observer*, 5th October, 1915
22   *Nuneaton Observer*, 3[1st] December, 1915
23   *Nuneaton Observer*, 17th September, 1915
24   *Nuneaton Observer*, 12th November, 1920
25   *Nuneaton Observer*, 27th May, 1921

15

After Gallipoli

cx

The area's fascination with the soldiers of the 29th Division did not end with their departure from the Gallipoli Peninsula in January 1916. Throughout the remainder of the war, news of the Division and its soldiers continued to appear in the newspapers. Often it was to record decorations awarded to men from the Division. These included another VC awarded to a man billeted in Rugby: on this occasion Sergeant Edward Mott, 1st Battalion Border Regiment, who was awarded the decoration for his bravery on the Western Front in January 1917. However, the continuing toll of casualties was also recorded. Among them was Sergeant James Somers VC: in July 1916, his wounding for the third time was reported and, in May 1918, came the news of his death, from the effects of gas inhalation.[1]

Soldiers continued to return to the area to visit friends they had made there or to further romances that had begun during the billeting period. Some of these stories can be glimpsed in the local newspapers; others have emerged through contact with the descendants of those involved.

On 25th April, 1916, a group of about 40 men from the Hampshire Regiment travelled to Stratford from Sutton Coldfield to attend a memorial service at the Parish Church. Those who were able to do so marched from the railway station to the church, with another half

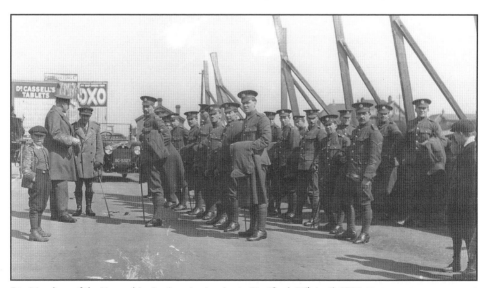

63. *Members of the Hampshire Regiment returning to Stratford; 25th April, 1916.* (© Shakespeare Birthplace Trust)

a dozen or so conveyed by motor car, on account of their wounds. The service, a year to the day after the landing of the 29th Division at Gallipoli, was conducted by Canon Melville. Those present included Mrs Carington Smith, widow of the 2nd Battalion's Commanding Officer. After the service, the soldiers were entertained at luncheon at the River Restaurant by the Mayor, Mr A.D. Flower.

In June 1916, Private Mulligan, 1st Battalion Royal Dublin Fusiliers, whilst on leave at Kenilworth, was interviewed by a representative of the *Coventry Herald*. Fourteen months had elapsed since he had been billeted in the town and he had much to reflect upon. The Gallipoli campaign had been followed by a spell in Egypt, as well as some time in very wet trenches on the Western Front. In the words of the reporter, Private Mulligan had experienced during his time away "more sights and sounds to stir the blood and torture the mind than are encompassed by an entire life of the normal comfortable, homely kind". Leave afforded him the first opportunity to sleep in a bed since leaving Kenilworth in March 1915. Of interest was his opinion that the Turk was a cleaner fighter than the German: "If the Englishman has used up his ammunition and takes to his bayonet, the Turk will do the same and there is a fair fight until one or other wins", whereas the German "funks the personal contact" and relies on his cartridge.[2]* A fortnight later, one of Mulligan's comrades, Lance-Corporal Thomas Griffin, also spent his leave in Kenilworth. The *Herald* used the story as an opportunity to emphasise the contribution that Ireland was making to the war effort, with more than 155,000 Irishmen serving with the forces.[3]

Not all returning soldiers were welcome. On 29th March, 1916, Edward Sterling appeared before Nuneaton Police Court, charged with being drunk and disorderly in Webb Street, Stockingford, and with damaging the property of Thomas Batchelor. Sterling was a former Royal Fusilier who had been wounded five times and discharged from the army with a pension. At about 9.30 p.m., on 28th March, he had called at the Batchelor household, the worse for drink, and demanded to see the daughter. A window was broken and he repeatedly tried to gain access to the house before he was arrested. He had been "keeping company" with Mr Batchelor's daughter, a liaison to which Mr Batchelor objected. The Bench ordered the prisoner to pay 5s damages but no conviction was recorded, in view of Sterling's military service and wounds. However, he was warned to keep away from the Batchelor household. The account of the 'Royal Fusilier and Stockingford Girl' appeared with double inverted commas around "Royal".[4]

A Royal Fusilier who was far more welcome was John Henry (Jack) Fordham. Originally from West Ham, Jack was the son of a signalman who worked on the railways in London's dockland. In June 1908, at the age of 17, he joined the 2nd Battalion Royal Fusiliers. After service in Ireland, the Battalion was sent out to India and took part in the 1911 Delhi Durbar, which was held in celebration of King George V's coronation. The Battalion was at Calcutta when war broke out and from there it made the long journey back to England. At Stockingford, Jack Fordham and his friend, Will Murray, were billeted at 36 Grove Road, the home of Joseph Neale, a miner, and his wife, Hannah. Four of the six Neale children were still living at home, so the addition of two soldiers to the household must have made it very crowded. However, the arrangements worked well, with regular sing-songs around the family piano. Will Murray, who had been brought up in an orphanage, enjoyed a normal 'family' life for the first, and sadly only, time in his short life. Jack Fordham impressed 10

---

* As such, his views reflect the increasing respect that many British soldiers had for their Turkish opponents. Whilst stories of the Turks being cowardly and resorting to treacherous tactics remained throughout the campaign, there were also increasing numbers of tributes to their courage, albeit some rather back-handed ones: "The Turk is not a bad soldier ... he attacks very regularly, only to be mown down."

64. *Jack Fordham of the 2ⁿᵈ Battalion Royal Fusiliers: "a very smart looking young man".* (© David Fordham)

65. *Jack Fordham and Kitty Neale.* (© David Fordham)

year-old Annie Cecilia Neale as being "a very smart looking young man, and had very nice manners". He also impressed Annie's elder sister, Catherine (Kitty), who was working at the time as a seamstress with Messrs Hart and Levy in Nuneaton, and who celebrated her 21st birthday in January 1915. The attraction was mutual and Jack returned during the war, when leave permitted, to spend time with Catherine. For several months in 1917, he was convalescing from shrapnel wounds, and this was followed by a spell of instructional duty at Mansfield that afforded further opportunities for the couple to meet. Jack survived the war and was discharged with the rank of Sergeant. He returned to Stockingford and he and Catherine were married in August 1919. They subsequently raised a family in Stockingford and, from 1925, lived in a house in Arbury Road, almost opposite the no longer extant Conservative Club, which had served as the 2ⁿᵈ Battalion headquarters in 1915 and which then became Jack's 'local'. He held a variety of jobs in the Nuneaton area and served in the Home Guard during World War II, doubling as a uniformed and armed guard at Rist's Wires and Cables. Jack's billeting partner, Private William Murray, had been killed on the opening day of the Battle of the Somme, 1st July 1916, and is commemorated on the Thiepval Memorial.[5]

Another soldier who returned to Nuneaton whenever he could was Private Martin Chasty, 1st Battalion Lancashire Fusiliers. He had been billeted in Broad Street with a Mrs Spencer. He had no relatives and now saw Nuneaton as his home. He had just returned to France, after a short furlough at his old billet, when he was wounded during the fighting that was part of the German spring offensive in 1918. He died on 15th April at the 56th General Hospital and was buried at Etaples Military Cemetery. The pathos of his story

66. *The names of Robert Bushill and Martin Chesty (also known as Chasty, Cheasty and Chaisty) on the Riversley Park war memorial in Nuneaton. Both came to Nuneaton during the billeting period in 1915 and found a home in the town.* (© Author)

– "homeless, friendless, and with no relatives in all the wide world", according to the *Nuneaton Observer* – struck a chord and it would seem that his name was subsequently added to the Nuneaton War Memorial. At least that appears to be the only explanation for the inclusion on the memorial of 'Pte M. Chesty, Lancashire Fusiliers'. Uncertainty surrounded Martin's surname name, which also appears as 'Cheasty' ('Soldiers Died') and 'Chaisty' (Commonwealth War Graves Commission).

Robert William Bushill's name is also on the Nuneaton Memorial. From Acton, in London, Robert Bushill (who seems to have been known as 'Will' in the family), was billeted in Stockingford with the 2nd Battalion of the Royal Fusiliers. There he met Helen ('Nell') Yeatman. Robert subsequently landed at Gallipoli with the 29th Division, on 25th April, 1915. Although his service papers have not survived, it seems that he was either wounded at Gallipoli or became ill, and was sent home to recuperate. On his recovery, he was drafted to the Royal Fusiliers' 3rd Battalion, which had arrived at Salonika in December 1915. However, before he joined his new battalion, he and Helen married at St Paul's Church, Stockingford, on 7th March, 1916. In November, Robert was again invalided away from the theatre of war. As the 3rd Battalion had not yet done much by way of fighting, Robert was more likely to have been suffering from illness, quite probably malaria, which was widespread. The Regimental history records that "drafts reaching the country seemed to be attacked almost on arrival".[6] Whatever the cause, Robert was on the Hospital Ship *Braemar*, bound for Malta, when it struck a mine, just off the island of Tinos, in the Aegean Sea. The ship was beached and subsequently repaired. Five men died in the incident: four members of the crew and Robert Bushill, the only patient who was lost. He is commemorated on the Mikra Memorial, in Greece, the Nuneaton Memorial and also on the memorial in St Paul's Church, Stockingford, where he and Helen had been married.[7]

Band Sergeant John Golding was a member of the 1st Battalion Lancashire Fusiliers. He served an estimated 24 years in the army, surviving both the Gallipoli campaign and the fighting on the Western Front. However, he was discharged from the army before the end of the war and, "having no home of his own", came back to Nuneaton, where he had "a large circle of friends". For a while, he lived in the Coton area of the town. Sadly, he fell victim to tuberculosis and died at Nuneaton Poor Law Infirmary on 7th January, 1919, at the age of 38. His funeral at Nuneaton Cemetery was witnessed by a large gathering, with soldiers from Warwick playing the last post and discharging a volley over his grave. Among the floral tributes was one with the inscription: "In memory of an old comrade, from the few survivors of the 1st Lancashire Regiment now residing at Nuneaton."[8]

A happier story was that of Corporal Arthur Gridley, 1st Battalion Lancashire Fusiliers, who married Frances Wilson, of Duke Street, Nuneaton, at the Abbey Church, on 12th January, 1917. Arthur had been wounded twice at Gallipoli but survived the war. Another Nuneaton marriage was that of Captain J.M. Mood, 1st Battalion Royal Dublin Fusiliers, to the daughter of Sir William Wiseman. For the first few years of the war, Miss Wiseman had acted as secretary of the Nuneaton Branch of the Sailors' and Soldiers' Families' Association. During his time in Nuneaton, Captain Mood had been responsible for organising a number of concerts "for the benefit of charity and the amusement of his men". Whether this was the way in which he met his wife is not recorded. After the war the couple appear to have settled in Sussex because it was there that a son was born, the birth being recorded in the *Nuneaton Observer*, under the heading "Interesting Event. Sequel to War-Time Romance."[9]

In Coventry, Private Bob Jordan had been billeted with the 1st Battalion Royal Munster Fusiliers. Recruited into the Regiment by their father, Bob and his brother Peter had finished their time with the colours and were living in the United States when war was declared. Nonetheless, they returned and joined the 1st Battalion in Coventry. It was there that Bob met Elsie Flemming. She was 21 years old and was convalescing from a cycling accident. Before the Regiment left Coventry, Bob went to see Elsie at the nursing home, charming his way past the matron and asking Elsie if she would wait for him. Elsie's reply was guarded: she said that she would not promise but that she would be straight with him and let him know if she met someone else. Bob was wounded twice at Gallipoli and returned to Coventry to marry Elsie in 1917. He fought on the Western Front and survived the war. Peter was less fortunate: he died of wounds on 30th May, 1918. Bob and Elsie raised a family in Coventry, sadly losing their eldest son in the Second World War, killed whilst serving in the Merchant Navy. Their other son, Tony, lived for many years with his family on the London Road, at Stretton on Dunsmore, a few hundred yards from the memorial to the 29th Division.[10]

67. *Elsie and Bob Jordan on their wedding day in 1917.* (© Tony Jordan)

In Rugby, Thomas Ash had served with the Border Regiment and returned to marry Eleanor Garlick, on Christmas Day, 1917. After the war, he and Eleanor settled in Rugby and raised a family. Thomas found employment with the Rugby Corporation and worked for 13 years as a grave digger. He became a member of the local branch of the British Legion and was involved in the local Boy Scout movement. He was killed, in February 1935, at the age of 49, when the grave he was digging in Clifton Road Cemetery collapsed and he was buried alive by an estimated three tons of earth. Even for a former soldier from a division that suffered more than 94,000 casualties during the First World War, it seems a particularly sad end. Thomas Ash's funeral service was conducted by the Venerable J.W. Hunkin, O.B.E., M.C., the Rector of Rugby and a former padré of the 29th Division.[11]

68. *The wedding of Thomas Ash and Eleanor Garlick, Rugby; Christmas Day, 1917.* (© Jerry Ash)

CB

1   *Rugby Advertiser*, 11th May, 1918. Somers died at home in Ireland.
2   *Coventry Herald*, 2nd/3rd June, 1915
3   *Coventry Herald*, 16th/17th June, 1916
4   *Nuneaton Observer*, 31st March, 1916
5   I am indebted to David Fordham for this information about his parents and also about William Murray.
6   H.C. O'Neill: "The Royal Fusiliers in the Great War"; William Heinemann, 1922
7   I am indebted to Anne Gore for the story of her great aunt Nell and Robert Bushill.
8   *Nuneaton Observer*, 17th January, 1919
9   *Nuneaton Observer*, 27th July, 1920
10 I am indebted to Tony Jordan for this information about his family. Further details can be found in "The Story Behind The Monument" by Chris Holland and Tony Jordan, Stretton Millennium History Group, 2005.
11 I am indebted to Jerry Ash for providing me with information on his grandparents and on the circumstances in which Thomas Ash died.

16

The Memorials

ɔB

The Eltham Memorial

The idea of a permanent memorial to commemorate the 29th Division was first suggested in the *Coventry Graphic* of 26th March, 1915. It reported a proposal for a memorial stone to mark the spot where the King inspected the Division and said that a letter had been written to the Chairman of the Warwickshire County Council in support of the idea.

However, the first memorial to the 29th Division to be unveiled was at Holy Trinity Church, Eltham, in London, on 25th April, 1917, the second anniversary of the Gallipoli landings. It commemorated those from the Division who died in the Gallipoli campaign and was paid for by the officers, men and friends of the Division. It takes the form of a carved oak reredos and side panelling, together with a figure of St George, and was unveiled by General Sir Ian Hamilton, the Commander in Chief of the Mediterranean Expeditionary Force, who paid tribute not only to the Division's losses at Gallipoli but also to its continuing work in France. Although three hundred percent of the Division's men had "gone under during the Gallipoli Campaign", their spirit, he said, lived on among the young soldiers who had replaced them: "Fortunate indeed the Commander-in-Chief who has such troops under his orders!"[1] The link between the Division and Eltham was provided by Henry Hall, Vicar of Holy Trinity Church, 1907-1942, who also served as Chaplain to the 29th Division during the Gallipoli Campaign. Following his demobilisation in April 1916, he was determined to create a memorial to those from the Division who did not return and he transformed the St Agnes Chapel at Holy Trinity into the Gallipoli Memorial Chapel. From 1921 onwards, an annual memorial service has been held at the Church.

The Dunchuch Avenue

In December 1915 and March 1916, gales brought down 74 of the majestic elm trees in the avenue along the London Road, which had been the line of inspection on 12th March, 1915. The state of the windfalls helped convince the Duke of Buccleuch's representatives that many of the other elms were in a "rotten and dangerous state" and should be felled, as they constituted a danger to the travelling public. It was not considered that lopping or pollarding the remaining trees would be sufficient to preserve them. On 15th June, 1917, and again on 8th January, 1918, Mr Cyprian Knollys, the Duke's Agent, wrote to the Warwickshire County Council outlining two possible courses of action. The first involved the felling of the avenue, with the Duke donating half the proceeds of the sale of the timber, after expenses had been deducted, to the County Council, or another approved body. The money would then be used for replanting and the upkeep of the avenue. The second scheme was that the trees would be sold to the County Council, or approved body, at the rate of 6d per cubic foot, on condition that an avenue was kept up. It was considered that the sale price of the trees was half their real value. In each case, the Duke agreed to give up his rights on the unenclosed land on which the trees stood. The Duke expressed himself in favour of the first scheme, on the grounds that the planting of young trees alongside mature trees might not be successful, with the younger trees being shaded out, or damaged by the fall of the older trees or limbs from them. Mature trees left isolated by the loss of adjacent trees were themselves more prone to damage by high winds. A new avenue would pose fewer risks to road users and reduce damage to telephone wires.

The prospect of the historic avenue being felled provoked widespread opposition, with several individuals and local councils expressing their concern. Thus the unanimous resolution of the Rugby Rural District Council, who managed to combine protest with deference:

> "The Rugby Rural District Council has learned with deep regret that it is your gracious intention to cut down the elm trees which form the avenue on the Rugby and Coventry Road. As this avenue is so widely known as one of the most beautiful in Warwickshire, and is also of historical interest, the Council hopes that your Grace may be induced to reconsider your decision and to allow the trees to remain."[2]

Coventry Council expressed its "deep concern" at the proposed destruction of "this glorious avenue – one of the natural beauties of Warwickshire".[3] Warwick Town Council pointed out the connection between the avenue and the inspection of the 29th Division; they felt that the proposed monument to the Division would be "robbed of historic and picturesque surroundings".[4] The Councils of Coventry and Leamington, as well as Rugby Urban District Council, also submitted resolutions. Bilton Parish Council was among the smaller councils who joined the protest, arguing that the proposed felling of the trees would be "a national disaster". Understandably, there were some who were concerned that the decision was also influenced by the Duke's conviction that "the national need required the timber", even

69. *"It has dignity": the Dunchurch Avenue, near Stretton on Dunsmore. News that the Avenue might be felled caused a local outcry in 1917 and 1918.* (© David Fry)

70. *Gale damage to the Dunchurch Avenue: the London Road between the 'Blue Boar' and Stretton on Dunsmore, 1916.* (© Warwickshire Library and Information Service)

though the trees were elm and not the more useful ash.[5] The *Coventry Herald*, beneath a picture of "The Famous Dunchurch Avenue", reported the approaches to the Duke "to avert what anyone with a real sense of the value of things would be compelled to regard as a disaster of more than local gravity. Dunchurch Avenue is entitled to veneration. … There is something of the aristocracy of Nature about it. It has dignity."[6]

The Duke's proposed options were considered first by the newly formed Dunchurch Avenue Committee. The Committee was chaired by Alderman Captain Oliver Bellassis and its 16 members included Lord Algernon Percy, Chairman of the Warwickshire County Council, J.J. McKinnell, Chairman of Rugby Urban District Council, and the Mayors of Coventry, Nuneaton, Leamington Spa, Warwick and Stratford. Mr E. Field, Clerk to the County Council acted as Secretary and Mr F.R. Davenport was the honorary organiser. The Committee expressed the opinion that scheme No. 2 should be adopted, if sufficient money could be raised. Part of the difficulty with this option, however, was that the County Council had no powers to purchase the trees, although they could receive them as custodians. In the event, at a meeting on 30th January, 1918, the Warwickshire County Council rejected the Committee's recommendation and voted in favour of scheme No. 1: the felling and replanting of the avenue.[7] The argument for preservation had been lost. As proposed, the Duke agreed to give up his rights to the unenclosed land upon which the trees stood and to donate half the proceeds from the sale of the felled timber. In return, the Committee agreed that the County Council would undertake to replant the avenue, which would serve as a living memorial to the 29th Division.[8]

From these discussions, it is apparent that, by the beginning of 1918, the idea (generally attributed to Coventry) of a "memorial stone" on the spot where the King took the salute had become accepted, along with the idea that the newly planted avenue would be part of the memorial – a proposal keenly advocated by the *Rugby Advertiser*. It was pointed out that the new avenue would be in its prime 100 years after the date of his Majesty's inspection. However, public subscription would be necessary to cover the costs of the memorial and the costs of replanting not covered by the Duke's donation from the sale of the timber. £5,000 was identified as the sum required. The breakdown was: £500 for the monument, £500 for alterations to the road system near the monument, £2,500 to cover the costs of replanting and a further £1,500 towards maintenance.[9] Public subscriptions were invited.* The Avenue Committee was retained and instructed to continue its activities with respect to the scheme adopted.

In the early autumn of 1918, the trees were submitted to public auction and acquired by a timber merchant from Arley, near Nuneaton, for £1,700, which was the maximum price allowed by wartime controls.

> "The work of cutting down was commenced at once, and before the end of the year every tree was lying low. The wide margins on each side of the road, strewed with the massive boles, the lop and top and other debris, presented a weird and regretful picture, conveying a mild idea, perhaps, of what has happened to many of the well-timbered parts of France and Belgium."[10]

There was a widespread feeling that the task of felling was taken too far and that more discrimination could have been shown. Along with the elms, a number of perfectly sound trees, including chestnuts and sycamores, had been cleared away. The purchaser of the trees was given until October 1919 to remove the timber. £720 was donated by the Duke to the appeal from the sale of the timber.

During the winter of 1920-21, two miles of the avenue were replanted. The original proposal for a mixture of trees, which included Canadian poplars, red chestnuts and scarlet oaks, was rejected in favour of a greater number of trees from native species. Thus, lime trees were planted at the Coventry end of the avenue and beech at the Dunchurch end, where Montana elm trees were also included. Altogether, some 470 young trees were planted.

The Monument

The monument was designed by Bridgeman and Sons, of Lichfield and was erected late in 1920. It takes the form of an obelisk 39 feet 9 inches high (12.3 metres), made out of Portland Stone and standing on a substantial base. The main inscription is on the north-facing panel, with the Divisional sign, the flattened red triangle, beneath. The pedestal contains the Division's "Order of Battle on Leaving England, March 1915." Originally, the monument stood on a gentle grass mound and was flanked by two German guns, still with their camouflage paint, which bore the inscription "Captured by the 29th Division on Sept. 28th, 1918, when advancing from Ypres to Menin." To allow greater room for the monument and the guns, some alteration to the road system was made, with a new corner being cut into the Fosse Way on the east side of the memorial. To the regret of local children, the guns were removed for scrap during the Second World War.† The mound was levelled, it is assumed, at the time of the changes to the road system in the late 1950s.

---

* In the event, only £2,234 17s 7d was raised, including subscriptions of £1,514 17s 7d. However, this was sufficient to cover the costs of the scheme and to leave a modest surplus. (County Surveyor's Department: War Memorial Correspondence; Warwickshire County Record Office, CR 2217/6/1-386)

† Inevitably, the guns provided an attraction for local children and the monument also seems to have been a popular halt for cyclists in the inter-war period. A widespread local story is that a German shell was found in the breach of one of the guns when it was being dismantled, although this seems rather unlikely, and is refuted by those who claim that you could see daylight when you looked up the barrels from the breach end. Another story recounted to the author is that the dismantling of one of the guns activated the recoil mechanism of the (now detached) barrel, which was propelled across the London Road. It is understood that the guns were taken to Rugby to be melted down.

71. The unveiling of the monument; Empire Day, 24th May, 1921. (© Warwickshire County Record Office)

72. *The unveiling of the monument; Empire Day, 24ᵗʰ May, 1921.* (© Albert Smith)

The monument was unveiled on Empire Day, Tuesday 24th May, 1921. It was, of course, a time of commemoration and, three days before, another distinctive local memorial was unveiled at Meriden, this being in memory of the cyclists, or "wheelmen", who had fallen in the war.

A crowd, variously estimated at between 7,000 and 10,000, began to assemble at the crossroads, near Stretton on Dunsmore, shortly after 1 p.m., two hours before the ceremony was timed to commence. Women seem to have been predominant and included those "dressed in the latest Paris gowns, others in simple country garb". An enclosure was reserved for members of the County Council and subscribers to the funds. Two smaller enclosures were set aside for former members of the 29th Division and for ex-soldiers from Warwickshire. The latter formed up on a field and were cheered by the crowd as they marched to their position. The guard of honour was provided by the Warwickshire Yeomanry, who also provided the band. The monument was unveiled by the Lord Lieutenant of Warwickshire, Earl Craven, who handed it over to Lord Algernon Percy, Chairman of the Warwickshire County Council. As the Union flag was released, the

73. *The monument shortly after its unveiling in 1921, flanked by two captured German guns. The guards around newly planted trees are visible in the background.* (© Warwickshire Library and Information Service)

band played the General Salute, the military present stood at the salute and the crowd bared their heads. The Lord Bishop of Coventry offered up a prayer, after which the hymn "Fight the Good Fight" was sung. In his speech, Lord Percy said that, during their stay, the Division had endeared themselves to the inhabitants of Warwickshire by their discipline and excellent conduct. He quoted Lord Kitchener, who had described the Division as the finest body of troops that had ever left the country.

Those present included Major-General D.E. Cayley, who had commanded the Division for part of 1918, and General Sir Ian Hamilton. Cayley said that he regretted the absence of more famous officers, notably General Hunter-Weston and General Beauvoir de Lisle, but felt that he had one qualification that they did not, namely that he had been present at the King's inspection on 12th March, 1915. He spoke movingly of the time that the Division had spent in the area:

74. *Lieutenant-Colonel D.E. Cayley, Commanding Officer 4th Battalion Worcestershire Regiment in 1915; General Officer Commanding the 29th Division in 1918.* (© Worcestershire Regiment Museum)

"It was the friendship, the hospitality, and the kind welcome you gave us when we were billeted among you, that materially helped us feel that old England was really a country worth dying for."

Sir Ian Hamilton described the memorial as "part living in its avenue of trees, part dead in its stonework", just like the incomparable Division in whose honour it stood, "a few of them still alive, most of them 'gone west'". He made reference to the terrible casualties suffered at Gallipoli, "wiped out three times over", and praised the Division's tenacity:

"If you want to see a monument raised to tenacity, you must not go to the Dardanelles. Come here to Warwickshire and look here. … The 29th Division had come here on a three month visit in 1915: now they are here to stay."

The ceremony concluded with the singing of the National Anthem. Several wreaths were laid at the foot of the obelisk, including one from the villagers of Stretton on Dunsmore and another from "Your comrades throughout the great adventure and your friends."[11]

The Continuing Story

The avenue has experienced a troubled life since its replanting in 1920-21. The dry summer of 1921 contributed to a very high failure rate, with more than 80% of the trees in need of replacement. The beech trees, in particular, had fared very badly and were replaced with lime. Further replanting was carried out, on a reduced scale, throughout the 1920s. Strong winds damaged some of the trees and there were cases of vandalism, sufficiently serious for notice boards to be erected in 1924 offering a £5 reward for information leading to the conviction of anyone damaging the trees.‡ The widening of the carriageway in the

---

‡ However, a claim made in 1943 by a member of the 29th Division Association, that the main inscription on the monument had been defaced, proved less sinister. In 1940, at a time when signposts were being taken down, the centre panel had been covered with a rendering of weak mortar, so as to deny invading Germans the knowledge that they stood "at the centre of England where Telford's coaching road … is crossed by the Roman Fosse Way"! The rendering was subsequently removed and the lettering reinstated. (County Surveyor's Department: War Memorial Correspondence; Warwickshire County Record Office, CR 2217/6/1-386)

75. *A ceremony at the monument to the 29th Division in 1939.* (© Warwickshire Library and Information Service)

interwar period restricted the development of many trees, as did unchecked outgrowth from adjacent hedges. In 1953, when Mr W.M. Campbell, Curator of the Royal Botanical Gardens, at Kew, was asked to report on the condition of the avenue, elm disease was affecting nearly 80 trees. Further problems included the low lying situation in which many trees had been planted, resulting in a waterlogged soil, and a major GPO line on the south side of the road. A number of trees had also been badly damaged by the proprietor of Autos café. Nonetheless, although Mr Campbell felt that the trees had not made the expected growth, he still hoped that the avenue could be maintained: "Nothing quite like this is to be found in any part of the country."[12]

In fact, the future for the avenue was no easier. In the late 1950s, the London Road (A45) was turned into a dual carriageway, resulting in the loss of trees on the south side of the avenue, with some replacement planting along the south side of the new carriageway. In the 1970s, disease ravaged the country's elm trees. In 1984, a large traffic island was constructed to improve the junction of the London Road and the Fosse Way, the scene of several fatal road accidents. This left the monument isolated on the new island, although the island is large enough to include several lime trees.

Ceremonies were conducted at the monument during the inter-war period – see Illustration 75. In more recent times, Jim Pawsey, the MP for Rugby, was behind a ceremony held on Sunday, 25th April, 1993. He was determined to renew interest in the heroism of the soldiers of the 29th Division and was assisted in his arrangements by Fred Watson, Chairman of the Warwickshire County Council, and by the Stretton on Dunsmore Parish Council. The service, which took place on the anniversary of the Division's landing at Gallipoli, was attended by more than 150 people and was addressed by representatives of the Anglican, Roman Catholic and Free Churches. Jim Pawsey expressed the hope that the upkeep of the monument and the island upon which it is now situated might be improved. In 2001, Stretton on Dunsmore Parish Council, supported by a generous donation of £14,000 from RMC Aggregates, were able to proceed with the refurbishment of the memorial and a service of re-dedication was held on 23rd September, 2001. The solemnity of the occasion was enhanced by the presence of the Dunchurch Silver Band, who had also participated in the 1993 ceremony, and by members of the Coventry and District Standard Bearers.

In March 2000, the Gallipoli Association held a ceremony to mark the 85th anniversary of the King's inspection. The proceedings were headed by Commander Henry Brooke, the son of Major George Brooke, 1st Battalion Border Regiment, who had been killed at Gallipoli on 28th April, 1915. This was the first of what have become annual ceremonies organised by the Gallipoli Association; they are held each March on a Sunday close to the anniversary of the King's inspection on 12th March, 1915. The villagers of Stretton on Dunsmore incorporate a service at the monument in their observance of Remembrance Sunday and others who have held ceremonies there include the Western Front Association in November 2007 and the Royal Dublin Fusiliers Association in October 2008.

Sadly, the hope expressed when the avenue was replanted in 1920-21, that it would look at its best in time for the centenary of the King's inspection, has not been fulfilled. Moreover, the upkeep of the island upon which the monument now stands has sometimes been neglected and has called for vigilance on the part of those who count the matter important. Nonetheless, the prediction made in 1921 by Major-General Cayley has survived. Looking at the monument, he said that:

"as long as any of the 29th Division live, this place will be a place of pilgrimage for them, and long after all were gone it will be a place of pilgrimage for their sons and their sons' sons. And on this spot, where the spirit of the Division was first made in this county, that spirit will be handed down from generation to generation, helped most tremendously by this memorial."

೦ಜ

1   *Rugby Advertiser*, 28th April, 1917

2   *Rugby Advertiser*, 10th November, 1917

3   *Nuneaton Observer*, 16th November, 1917

4   *Rugby Advertiser*, 17th November, 1917

5   *Rugby Advertiser*, 10th November, 1917.

6   *Coventry Herald*, 30th November / 1st December, 1917

7   *Coventry Herald*, 1st/2nd February, 1918

8   *Rugby Advertiser*, 2nd February, 1918

9   *Rugby Advertiser*, 30th May, 1919

10 *Rugby Advertiser*, 14th February, 1919

11 *Coventry Herald* 27th/28th May, 1921; *Nuneaton Observer*, 27th May, 1921; *Rugby Advertiser*, 27th May, 1921

12 County Surveyor's Department: War Memorial Correspondence; Warwickshire County Record Office, CR 2217/6/1-386

More recent ceremonies organised by:

76. *The Gallipoli Association, 2005.* (© Author)

77. *The Royal Dublin Fusiliers Association, 2008.* (© Author)

78. *"The 29th Division came here on a three month visit in 1915: now they are here to stay."* (© David Fry)

Index

❧

Military Units:

Warwickshire Great War Publications

Established in 2012 to encourage and to publish research into the impact of the Great War on the Coventry and Warwickshire area. Already published:

A Strange Time: The Diary and Scrapbooks of Cordelia Leigh, 1914-1919
Sheila Woolf and Chris Holland
2012

In August 1914, Cordelia Leigh, who described herself as "a private individual living at Stoneleigh Abbey", decided to keep "a short record of this time of war". Her wartime diary and accompanying scrapbooks chronicle her experiences and thoughts during the Great War, along with those of her family, friends and local villagers. Published for the first time, the war diary of Cordelia Leigh is accompanied by extracts from her scrapbooks and a commentary by Sheila Woolf and Chris Holland. The book provides not only valuable insights into the impact of the Great War but also:

"a detailed picture of a remarkable woman" (Dr Philip Errington)

ISBN: 978-0-9574216-0-8 155 pages Illustrated £9.95

ଓ

Coventry and Warwickshire 1914-1919: Local Aspects of the Great War, Volume 1
Edited by Chris Holland
2012

Local historians explore major themes from the Great War to show how individuals and communities responded to the demands placed upon them by more than four years of war. The topics covered are:
August 1914 ~ Belgian refugees ~ recruitment in the early stages of the war ~ the billeting of soldiers ~ hospital provision for wounded soldiers ~ the expansion of industry ~ increasing food production ~ the 'war courts' ~ the impact of the 'Spanish' 'flu ~ the news of the Armistice

"a work of meticulous scholarship" (*Local History Magazine*)

"discussed with a telling and humane attention to the stories of individuals and families, while at the same time reminding the reader of how these experiences were a direct part of wider ... trends"
(Kate Tiller, *The Local Historian*)

ISBN: 978-0-9574216-1-5 160 pages Illustrated £9.95

ଓ

**Both books can be obtained direct from Chris Holland. Please contact him:
02476 542493 or poors_plot@tiscali.co.uk**